The Second Chance

[A SEGUNDA CHANCE]

Portuguese Version Included • Versão em Português incluída

Mira Sousa

Parsons Publishing House

Christiansburg, Virginia USA

The Second Chance
by Mira Sousa

Parsons Publishing House
Christiansburg, VA 24073 USA
www.ParsonsPublishingHouse.com
Info@ParsonsPublishingHouse.com

Printed in the United States of America.
For World-Wide Distribution.

ISBN -13: 978-1-60273-092-2
ISBN -10: 1-60273-092-X

English translation provided by Quezia Soares.

The real names have been changed to protect the privacy of those involved.

Os nomes verdadeiros foram alterados para preservar a identidade dos envolvidos.

DEDICATION

To the One who always gives a second chance: God.

MY DEEPEST THANKS AND GRATITUDE

To the Lord Jesus Christ: My true friend—faithful in the battle.
To my family: You have been my source of inspiration.
To my beloved Church: ***Jesus Christ is Life***, which has supported me so much in difficult times.
To my sisters in Christ from the prayer circle here in Brazil and the prayer circle Lily of the Valley, in the United States. They have sustained me with their love and care.
To Selma Alves, who strengthened me with her precious prayers over the phone.
To Celia Feldpausch, for her encouragement and valuable prayers.
To my dear sister Quezia, who took care of this book's word processing.
To the Parsons family, for graciously publishing this work.

My gratitude,
Missionary Mira Sousa

TABLE OF CONTENTS

FOREWORD

When I came to live in my apartment in 2009, I heard about a sister who did a beautiful job with the children in her home. However, she was then living in the United States. Sometime later, I met sister Mira during one of her visits to Brazil.

My first impression of her was about a very unassuming person. As I heard her preach, I realized that she was a servant of God who truly knew her Lord. I only knew the details of her life when I was invited to type the manuscript of her book. In it, the author presents a God who is personal and intimate with those who seek Him, unlike the distant and indifferent God that many people worship. Throughout the book, she highlights how God is good and merciful. Her grateful heart gives glory to this wonderful God during all of the narrative.

There is no apologia for prosperity or for having material goods. But with great simplicity, she tells how God has supplied all her spiritual, material and emotional needs. In fact, just knowing sister Mira personally is enough to see that she does not boast riches. However, this book also makes clear that our God delights in blessing us and keeping His Word, which says that the righteous and His children will not beg for bread. And all of this is to glorify the name of the Lord, not because we are good, but because He is good to us.

The Second Chance also teaches us that before anything else, we need salvation. We must recognize that we are sinners and Jesus is the only one who can save us from eternal damnation. This Jesus is not the one made by human hands that many insist on worshiping in their spiritual blindness. But, He is the real Jesus who came to earth, died, rose again and lives.

Finally, each experience that is described in the book is a living testimony that will fill the reader's heart with hope in Jesus. Faith will grow with the assurance that "God sees everything you are going through, and nothing is hidden from His eyes. And at the right time, He will come with the help and deliverance you need" (Mira Sousa).

—Quézia Soares da Silva
Speech Therapist

INTRODUCTION

"Bless the Lord, O my soul: and all that is within me bless his holy name. Bless the Lord, O my soul, and forget not all his benefits" (Psalm 103:1-2, KJV).

When God revealed Himself to me through answers to prayer, I felt the desire to write a book that would lead people to know that God exists, that He is real and cares about his people.

You, my brother or sister in Christ, who are reading this book, should know that God sees everything you're going through, and nothing is hidden from His eyes. He will come in time with the help and deliverance you need. The confirmation for me to write this book came several years thereafter. When God has a plan in our life, it can take some time, but one day, what God has determined will come to pass.

In May of 2010, I was living in the United States and we were in a new church, which by the way, is very much alive. We had found new brothers and sisters. [1] The koinonia was very good. Since I was celebrating my birthday during that month, I asked my daughter Celina to prepare a party and a thanksgiving worship service. I wanted to thank God. She invited some friends, including the couple Darrell and Diane. Darrell was in the Air Force. He and his wife own a publishing company. But I did not know these details. Diane only speaks English and I speak only Portuguese. Our communication was minimal. Anyway, God had prepared everything. No one but God knew my desire to write a book. I kept it in my heart.

After the worship, Darrell asked me, "Can I pray for you?" I said yes. He prayed in English and my daughter, of course, translated it to me. Then Diane prayed and said, "I have a message from God to you. Do you want to hear?" When I said "yes," she started to say, "God has given you something that He wants you to share with people. He wants you to write a book. I will publish this book in the language of your choice."

I was amazed because the desire of my heart was being confirmed by the Lord, through Diane's word. It was my great birthday gift. For a long time I had wished to put my experience on paper and make known what God has done in my life. I wanted to tell what I learned throughout my walk with Him, since I've gotten to truly know Him. Although, I thought, "How can I write a book? I am no longer a young woman and I don't have a college degree. I am a foreigner here in this country (I was living in the United States of

America). Who will want to know my story?" And with so many questions, I was forgetting that it is God who empowers. We should not look at our inability because when God chooses someone to do His work, He empowers and gives the tools.

I confess that it took me a long time to decide to tell my life story.

> In that day it shall be said to Jerusalem, Fear thou not: and to Zion, Let not thine hands be slack. The Lord thy God in the midst of thee is mighty; he will save, he will rejoice over thee with joy; he will rest in his love, he will joy over thee with singing (Zephaniah 3:16-17, KJV).

This was the desire of my heart: to make known what God had done for me, and to glorify His name. If He did it for me, He can also do it for you. I thought that I was too ordinary to write a book. I gave all sorts of excuses, like Moses did when he was called by God to take the people out of Egypt and guide them to Canaan, the Promised Land.

> And Moses said unto the Lord, O my Lord, I am not eloquent, neither heretofore, nor since thou hast spoken unto thy servant: but I am slow of speech, and of a slow tongue. And the Lord said unto him, who hath made man's mouth? Or who maketh the dumb, or deaf, or the seeing, or the blind? Have not I the Lord? (Exodus 4:10-11, KJV).

Even with so many excuses, I started writing, and a writer was born. The one who had thought herself incapable of writing, had begun to write. I thought writing a book was like fighting a giant; however, the stone was accurately aimed at the giant's head, and here I am telling the story of my life to you.

[1]The word *koinonya* is used among Christians to designate communion between brothers.

1

MY HILLBILLY FAMILY

I was born in the 1940's, in Rio Grande do Norte—Brazil, in a city called Itabaiana, which is in the countryside. We had no electricity or transportation to go to the nearest towns—Itaipu and Baixa Verde. Our only means of transportation were horseback, donkey or riding in the back of a truck. The truck passed once a week, every Saturday morning. They picked up passengers in the morning and brought them back in the afternoon. Passengers spent the day in the city where they sold their products in the marketplace, such as cereal, molasses, cheese, chicken and other food. I remember that we looked forward to seeing daddy return, bringing back candies and something to eat.

I clearly remember my father with his straw hat and my mother with her hair tied behind her head in a bun and her chintz dresses with those large flowers. My mother had a soft face. She was very gentle, but when she got angry, I usually took off running. My family consisted of four people: my father, my mother, my sister Dora (who was always very shy), and me. Being the older sister, Dora was always my dad's favorite; however, when a visitor came to eat, she would always run and hide behind the house. Also, she didn't like to eat in front of anyone. Even today, she still does not like to eat with us.

Our house was very poor. It was made of clay and covered with tile. We had no furniture in the room, no bed, except for a wooden pallet that my parents used at night when sleeping. In the living room there was only a wooden bench where my father took his afternoon naps. We cooked with clay pots over a wood burning stove. My sister and I slept in hammocks, as is the custom in the Northeast of Brazil. One night, I woke up with a snake wrapped around the wrist of my hammock. Fortunately, it was not a poisonous snake. It was so scary!

My father was a farmer. He worked in the fields. He planted to eat. Since my father didn't like heavy work, we went through many difficulties. Our harvest was barely enough to feed us. I was thin and anemic. We had no dairy milk for the children. We had some meat from the chickens that we raised, and we made our own flour. A typical breakfast was cooked pumpkin or sweet potato, which was then mixed with coconut milk. No oil was used to prepare food. There was no table at my house. Mom put a tablecloth on the floor and we all sat around to eat. The light came from a kerosene lamp or a lantern.

I had only one dress, and it was ripped at the waist. I was always trying to tie up the top threads with the bottom to close the hole. I don't know why my mother never sewed it. I remember that she always looked unhappy and depressed about our state of poverty. When I took a shower, I needed to stay wrapped in a sheet waiting for my clothes to dry. When I was young, I had typhoid fever, and my hair fell out completely. Thank God I didn't have permanent complications.

My father was a tough man and full of quirks and superstitions. When my mom gave him coffee, he always looked into the cup to see the reflection of his face there. If he did not see it, he did not drink the coffee. My sister Dora and I had no toys. However, I loved pretending to cook food. Every time my mother killed a chicken, she would separate the gizzards for me to cook. My cooking pots were empty cans of canned meat that she kept for me. I have always loved to cook. Even today, everyone says that I cook very well.

As we say in Northeast Brazil, my father was moody. One day he was fine, the next, in a bad mood. I believe he was bipolar. When my father was happy, he played an instrument that he had made. It is similar to a "berimbau," which is essentially a pole with a string attached to it. My sister accompanied him with her tambourine made out of a guava paste can. We sat in front of our home and had a lot of fun. When I told my grandson, Jonathan, that I had no toys when I was a child, he went to his bedroom, grabbed some of his toys and said, "Look, Grandma, these are for you to play with, okay? Afterwards, you can give them back."

Our religion in Brazil was Roman Catholicism, but I do not remember attending even one church mass in my childhood. However, we prayed at home and we knew all the “saints” and traditions such as the Heart of Jesus, Hail Mary, Saint Severino of the Branch, Saint Damian and Father Cícero Romão Batista. We had some pictures of the saints on our walls, which is customary. Our dream was to go to the northeastern of Ceará to visit the priest Cícero Romão Batista. Father Batista died on July 20, 1934, in Juazeiro do Norte, Brazil, at the age of 90. He is buried in the Church of Our Lady of Perpetual Help. Many Catholics believe today that this priest performs miracles. This was great spiritual ignorance. How could a dead man do anything? In Ecclesiastes 9:5 we read, “For the living know that they shall die: but the dead know not anything, neither have they any more a reward; for the memory of them is forgotten.”

2

MY AUNT'S VISIT

When I was five years old, an aunt who lived in the capital of Rio Grande do Norte, Natal, came to visit us. Aunt Maria was her name. I remember as if it was yesterday. She was a nice lady with a round face, black hair tied in a bun, beady black eyes, thick eyebrows and a wide, kind smile. She wore a simple long-sleeved dress because she was from a Pentecostal Christian denomination. This aunt introduced me to Jesus, my Savior.

I loved Jesus, but the Jesus I knew was made of clay and wood. He was dead on the cross with a crown of thorns on his head and could not do anything for anyone.

> They have mouths, but cannot speak, eyes, but cannot see. They have ears, but cannot hear,

> noses, but cannot smell. They have hands, but cannot feel, feet, but cannot walk, nor can they utter a sound with their throats. Those who make them will be like them and so will all who trust in them" (Psalms 115:5-8).

As I did not know the living God, I was in this lifeless condition, which focuses on worshiping a false god who could do nothing for me. Praise the Lord who sent me my aunt to present the living, powerful, real and true God, who can help me in any trouble that I may go through. However, it took a long time for me to really know this living God, and have life experiences with Him.

My aunt told me that the Jesus I saw was made of wood, but there was one that was real. As a child, I kept her words in my heart. My friend, never miss the opportunity to present the Lord Jesus to people and tell about His love for us! I lived in the countryside. There was no evangelical church for me to attend. Besides, people spoke many things against the believers. They told lies about evangelicals. They spread a story that while Christians were kneeling and praying a "Jesus" with a tail walked in the midst of them. I don't know where this rumor came from. It could only be from our enemy. I didn't care about it. I kept what she told me. The gospel seed was planted in my heart, and stayed there until it was time to germinate and bear fruit for the glory of God.

My parents never knew that my aunt talked about her faith in Jesus to me. I heard people saying, "These believers, these goats!" There was a lot of prejudice and persecution. Thank God, today the gospel has more acceptance in Brazil.

3

FROM THE COUNTRYSIDE TO THE BIG CITY

When I was seven to eight years old my mother became very sick with typhoid disease, so my father brought a niece into our home to take care of us. In the course of time, he had an affair with this niece, and went away to live with her. My uncle, my mother's brother, knowing our difficult situation took us to the capital, Natal, where he lived. So, we went to live with my maternal grandparents.

The typhoid disease left my mother with side effects: a shortened leg. She started to walk with difficulty and limping. Our uncle helped us with the groceries and clothes. When there was someone looking for a house cleaner, my mother went to work to help with the expenses. She also liked to make coconut sweets and cakes to sell. As our income was low, at nine years of age, I went to work as a maid too.

When my mom left me at the first home where I worked, I cried a lot. I didn't want to stay away from her. On the weekends she picked me up. And so, my childhood was full of needs. I didn't know what it was like to be a child or to play without worry of not having enough to eat. My sister Dora married at seventeen, but her husband earned little and could not help us.

At that time, my grandfather died. My mother had gotten a job as a maid and I was living alone with my grandmother. Together we attended a very strict Pentecostal church. This was the type of church that didn't allow haircuts, lipstick, earrings or any kind of vanity. I could not even use deodorant. The dresses had to be long sleeved. Imagine this in the Northeast of Brazil where it is very hot most of the year. It was quite uncomfortable!

I was already a teenager and was starting to flirt. My uncle, who was very careful with me, thought that my grandmother could no longer take care of me. Then he handed me back to my mother. I had nowhere to live and we both lived with relatives. Every week we would go to a different house; we had no fixed place. We looked like a ping pong ball. I hated that situation. I wished to have my house, a place of my own, where I could have privacy.

I thought about getting married, but I was still very young. I thought that when I got married, everything should be fine. I discovered later that things are not quite like we think. It is good to get married and have a house of our own, but true happiness is only found in Jesus Christ, where we can take shelter under the shadow of His wings.

He will cover you with his feathers, and under his wings you will find refuge; his faithfulness will be your shield and rampart. He will call on me, and I will answer him; I will be with him in trouble, I will deliver him and honor him (Psalms 91:4, 15).

4

THE WORLD'S DECEPTION & FALSE JOY

When I was sixteen years old, my mother managed to rent a place for us to live. Mom had not yet become a believer. She only met Jesus later, when elderly. I did not have the support of a church nor of the brethren. I backslid away from the Lord and spent thirty years out of my Father's house. I turned away completely from the presence of God. I didn't understand that I had taken this step because of vanity and wanting to "enjoy" life, which would cost me a lot later. The Word of God says in Matthew 12:43-45:

> When an impure spirit comes out of a person, it goes through arid places seeking rest and does not find it. Then it says, 'I will return to the house I left.' When it arrives, it finds the house unoccupied, swept clean and put in

> order. Then it goes and takes with it seven other spirits more wicked than itself, and they go in and live there. And the final condition of that person is worse than the first. That is how it will be with this wicked generation.

That is what happened to me. I began consulting the horoscope, and I went to the fortune tellers as well as voodoo rituals. I danced in the famous clubs and when it was time for the carnival, I jumped in with both feet. I danced in "trios elétricos" through the streets. I also participated in a beauty pageant and won second place. I felt that I had the world at my feet.

I remember when I was in a club that had a bad reputation. It was not a place for a young family girl, but I was in rebellion. When friends invited me, I went everywhere with them. That day, it was one-thirty in the morning and I was in a place like that! Nobody cared about me. I mean nobody on Earth, but my Father in Heaven was watching me and spoke to me clearly in that place. I heard a voice inside me saying: "What are you doing here? This is not a place for you." Immediately, I grabbed my bag and went home alone, despite being the middle of the night.

I thought nobody cared about me, but there is a verse in the Bible that says, "Can a mother forget the baby at her breast and have no compassion on the child she has borne? Though she may forget, I will not forget you!" (Isaiah 49:15).

5

GOD TOOK CARE OF ME

In these modern times nobody has patience, or time to spend with others. In the age of computers and microwaves, everything is done in the fast lane. No time is set aside for prayer, to be alone with God and hear what He has to say. Consequently, the work of God suffers and Christians become weak as well as spiritually sick. They don't have the necessary spiritual food to grow strong and healthy. In Hosea 4:6 we read, "My people are destroyed for lack of knowledge."

Here in the United States there are theme parks called Busch Gardens. These gardens are amazing. Those who visit them can see their beauty, which fills the eyes. However, this is only possible because there are people watching, cleaning, pulling up weeds, watering and putting fertilizers suitable for their survival. There is a collective effort of people working to keep these gardens clean and beautiful.

Our spiritual lives are like a garden that needs care. If we are not careful, the enemy comes and sows weeds in our way without us noticing what is happening. In a short time we are weak, unwilling to read the Bible or even pray. It becomes boring to participate in the church services, everything seems to suffocate us. The enemy takes off the strength of the believer gradually, little by little. You don't even notice it.

Here goes an alert! If you start to have more pleasure in the things of the world than the things of God, beware! Put your knees to the ground immediately and ask the Lord for deliverance, strength and mercy. The enemy is just waiting for the right moment to make you fall into his trap.

When I was seventeen, my mother and I went to live in Rio de Janeiro. We left the Northeast and went to the Southeast of Brazil. Some relatives were already in Rio, and we joined them. I was very pretty, and coveted by young guys. I even got engaged and almost married. We stayed for a while in my cousin's house, but soon we rented our own place.

My mother went to work as a housemaid and I went to work as a nanny in Copacabana, a rich neighborhood. Copacabana has one of the most beautiful beaches in the southern part of Rio. It was then that I began to sink down to the deep. I spent Monday through Friday at work and on the weekends, I stayed with my family. I made many friends, and went without my family's supervision much of the time. I was free to do whatever I wanted. Unfortunately, that freedom cost me much suffering.

Copacabana was a beautiful beach, full of many attractions for a young girl with no experience and with little malice. Anyway, I was naive and trusted people. I had nobody to guide me through the world of illusions that I had come to know. It was in this paradise that I met Jefferson. He was a very handsome young man! He looked a lot like the Hollywood star, Tony Curtis. He had green eyes, black hair, and sun tanned skin. He was a Greek god!

I was enchanted by him. He had only one imperfection, he wasn't tall. But it didn't matter to me because I was short, too. I thought I was living a fairy tale. We only separated to go to work. I was very involved with him. However, I didn't know that my prince was possessive, violent and often drank. When we started dating, he did not reveal himself. This happened later.

When I realized what was happening, I was already pregnant. I almost had a conniption when I found out. What would my mother say? Nevertheless, God is wonderful and took care of me. When I told Jefferson that I was pregnant, he said: "Let's rent a place for us to live." I thank God that Jefferson didn't abandon me and actually accepted the situation.

However, that was not what I wanted. We moved in together without getting married, but I had always dreamed of getting married. My dream of marrying in the church, wearing a white wedding dress was lost. At that time, a woman could not wear a white wedding dress if she was living with a man or if she was pregnant. In this case, there could only be a simple civil marriage ceremony performed by a judge. However, even that was not to be.

He worked as an accountant and I worked in a shoe store. We lived in Copacabana. Our house was shared with another young man to help pay the rent. The situation was difficult because living in the southern suburbs was very expensive. We went without quite often. Many times we had to share a glass of avocado juice or a plate of bean soup for dinner. Despite the problems, I was happy. I thought I had found the perfect happiness.

At the time of my first pregnancy, Jefferson treated me with affection, helped me with the housework, and never went to bed without me. We were very close to each other. Everything seemed perfect. I didn't know that after my daughter's birth, everything would change. Celeste was born. She was beautiful! She looked like a child from a magazine cover.

Once I was stopped in the street and a girl asked: "What does your daughter eat? She is so beautiful!" Her mother, who was standing next to her, said, "She is not her mother! Can't you see that she is the girl's nanny?" I dedicated myself to that beautiful child, who arrived without being planned, but who was dearly loved by us.

I still wonder what happened to that happy and apparently perfect union. Five years later, I became pregnant with Celina. She was a feeble child with low birth weight. She cried a lot, but was also much loved by us. When she finished nursing, I would place her in the palm of my hands to burp. Then she would give me the most beautiful smile I've ever seen. She was a very tiny little girl, a living doll.

Even before Celina's birth, the disagreements, fights and verbal attacks had begun. The only reason there was no physical aggression was because I kept quiet and just cried. He abused me a lot, and did not permit my mother to see me. Therefore, I had no help with my household chores. I had to wash, iron, cook, and take care of the home with two daughters and a nephew who came from the countryside to live in our house. The nephew, seeing my difficult situation, often put Celina to sleep. When she was tired, she cried a lot until she fell asleep.

Due to our difficulties and not knowing what to do, I fell ill. I had panic attacks, depression, and fear. I didn't sleep because I thought that if I slept, I wouldn't wake up. I couldn't eat because everything made me sick. I weighed 80 pounds. I was afraid of taking medicine. I didn't watch television because I was afraid. I didn't want anyone to visit me. My life was a living hell. Many times I wanted to throw myself under a car, but I looked at my kids and thought, "they will suffer a lot if I do this." God didn't allow me to kill myself. I loved my children very much and didn't want them to suffer from my death. I can see now that God was taking care of me.

The Word of the Lord in Ecclesiastes 8:11 says: "When the sentence for a crime is not quickly carried out, people's hearts are filled with schemes to do wrong." I was reaping the result of my sin, my rebellion. Sin had drifted me away from the path of the Lord. I had gone to consult fortune-tellers, horoscope, occultists, and witchcraft. I had enjoyed what the world offers. Because I gave no heed to the holy and pure word of our beloved Savior Jesus Christ, I went through many afflictions and despair. I don't wish anyone to suffer at the hands of the devil like I did. Beloved, do not exchange Jesus for anything else. It's not worth it. Only in Him is peace, joy and perfect happiness. Don't leave Jesus out of your life.

6

TRYING TO GO BACK TO MY FIRST LOVE

After I went astray, I wanted to go back to Jesus, but had no strength. I was trapped by the wiles of the adversary. I spent thirty years away from the presence of God. Despite of all the suffering I went through, it still took a long time for me to realize that I needed to return to Jesus. God is wonderful, long-suffering and compassionate. His mercies are the reason that we are not consumed by our selfish desires. He is always ready to give us the opportunity to recognize our mistakes and repent as well as return to His presence. He always gives us a second chance.

My return to God's presence was very painful because satan didn't want to lose me, and he did everything to oppress me with fears, diseases and problems. Glory to God because when He chooses people, no one can snatch them from His hands. In Isaiah 43:13 we read, "Yes, and from ancient days I am He. No one can deliver out of My hand. When I act, who can reverse it?" This is what happened to me when I really decided to accept Jesus. It was a true conversion; however, I went back through much pain.

If you are reading this book and are away from the Lord, do not wait for the pain to bring you back to Him. Come for love! It's much better. When I went back to Jesus, I was still very weak and the Lord was healing me gradually. He healed me from splitting migraines. I started to eat and sleep better. But it still took five years for me to be restored completely.

Those were times of much surrender and many battles in our home because Jefferson did not accept my new faith. Many times, he arrived home drunk and breaking things in the house. Once he threatened me with a gun, so I had to lock myself in the bathroom. The kids were at the window calling for help. Thank God that He delivered me from the fury of that man. I was always afraid of something harmful happening to me or the kids.

One Sunday, I was leaving to go to church to teach Sunday School when he threw me on the floor and dragged me back into the house. Then he slammed the door and didn't let me go out. A neighbor came to ask him to let the children go and calm down; however, he didn't agree. We three sat on the couch afraid, and then I had an idea. I began to pray quietly for peace. He sat on the other couch away from us. When I looked, he was sleeping. When he woke up, he was calm and ashamed of what he had done. Afterwards, I discovered that he had a mistress, and spent many nights out of the house with her. He couldn't decide whether he would remain at home with me, or leave to be with her.

During this situation, I lived like a maid in my own house. I thought about taking a stand, and then I had a grand idea. Since he drank, I decided to pretend that I was drunk by emptying a bottle of Brazilian rum in the sink, and holding a cup of water in my hand when he came home. He was very frightened and said, “Are you crazy? You cannot drink! You’re a believer, and you’re going to get sick.” I had decided to give him a good scare. Aside from the cup with water and the bottle, I had a knife in my hand. He tried to take the knife from me, but I said, “Don’t get close to me, because I’m not in my right mind!” He sprawled on the sofa and didn’t come to the bedroom that night. When I woke up, he was still in the living room. The incident scared him so much that he had diarrhea for a whole week. Eventually, he decided to leave. Afterwards, I asked God for forgiveness for this very drastic attitude.

7

FINDING THE ALMIGHTY GOD

Despite being physically and mentally weak because of mistreatment, I enrolled in night school. I had studied only up to the fourth grade of elementary school. Fortunately, I finished night school. However, because of my poor health I had to stop taking the courses several times. One particular night, I went to bed. When I woke up in the morning and tried to sit on the bed, I couldn't, and fell to the side. It was as if my body lost balance. I couldn't sit, stand up, or walk. I searched for all of the doctors that I could, but nobody could figure out what I had. But Jesus had already prepared the cure for me. Glory to God for that! He was just waiting for me to return to Him without reserve. So I said, "Either to die or to live, I want to be with Jesus."

I was sad because I couldn't take care of my household chores. I had two small children to look after. Who would help me? I couldn't afford a maid and Jefferson said I had nothing wrong with me. He said that I was just faking being sick. At that time I had a dream. I dreamed that I answered the phone and then someone said, "I came to bring you good news." I didn't know that the word "gospel" means "good news." I was worried and thought, "Will I die? Could this call be a warning from another world to me?" This, I thought in my spiritual ignorance. A person who has moved on to the other world cannot communicate with us.

Thank God I didn't die, but God gave me a second chance to know Him better. Since then, I have had many wonderful experiences with Him, and see how great He truly is. At the night school where I was taking courses, I met Marilene, and soon we became friends. This friend was like an angel sent by God in my life. Marilene was a Christian and attended a deliverance worship service near her house.

During one of my sicknesses, she came to visit me, and asked if I wanted to go to a prayer meeting near my house. I said yes, but I couldn't walk. The sister who was the leader told Marilene that God wanted me to be there. I told Marilene: "How can I go there if I am not able to walk?" The sisters were praying for me, so that I would be able to get there.

After a month since Marilene invited me to the deliverance worship service (the sisters were praying for me throughout this month), I could finally go to the service and had a real encounter with my God after the prayer. My health improved gradually from that day forward. Almost five years later, I fully recovered. Jesus saved me, healed me, restored my self-esteem, and gave me great experiences with Him. Praise the Lord for his goodness.

That was a deliverance worship service attended by Spirit-filled Baptists and Pentecostals. When the service ended, a sister made an altar call to those who wanted to accept Jesus as their Savior. I was quiet on my corner seat, only hearing her say, "Accept Jesus!" She kept talking about accepting Jesus. That insistence was irritating me. I thought, "I will raise my hand so this woman will shut up!" I was still resisting the call to renew my life with God. In His great mercy, God took my hand. From that moment on, I came under the care of the Lord Jesus Christ. Hallelujah! I lifted my hand to Him. It was the best decision I made in my whole life!

8

OUT OF DARKNESS

When I had that encounter with Jesus in that service, I was still living with my partner. We had been together for twenty-one years. I stood firm with the Lord for two years before the father of my daughters left. When Jefferson found out I was going to church, he began to persecute me. Then, other trials started. He did not want me to go to church. I had to go in hiding.

Beloved, there were many persecutions. He said I was running after the pastor. When we lacked something at home and I spoke to him about it, the answer was: "Go ask the pastor." But, I persevered in seeking God. Jesus gave me victory! Hallelujah! I was very much in love with Jesus. Everywhere I went I gave away Bible tracks, and told people what He had done for me. How merciful He had been toward me.

After three months of participating in the prayer meetings with the sisters, I became a tither and gave offerings. The leader called me to go on home visits with her; she also gave me the opportunity to praise and even pray. Soon, Celina became a believer and assisted me with the visits.

Once I went out with the sisters to visit some people. When I arrived at the meeting place, they had already left, so I returned home. When I entered the hallway of my apartment block, some children came running and screaming for help. "There's a crazy woman and we are afraid to go home." I went to see what was happening. This lady was working as a maid for a neighbor in our building. I approached and asked, "What is going on, Ms. Maria?" And the answer came from a strange voice: "I am not Ms. Maria! What are you doing here? Darkness does not mix with light." I looked back to see if there was anyone else around us, but there was no one besides my daughter Celina. I realized that the lady was possessed by evil spirits. I had no experience in casting out demons (exorcism or deliverance).

Even with my little wisdom, I commanded them to leave that body in the name of the Lord Jesus. That lady fell to the ground, but it was a lot of work to get those demons out. There were many spirits, and there came a time when they said, "We're going to take her to the street and throw her under the car." So I said: "You are tied with your hands behind your back." She put her hands back as if she was physically tied. I was getting so tired of sending those demons away only to have them return. There were so many. I suddenly had an idea. I asked: "What are you doing here?" The spirits answered in regard to the lady, "She goes to Church and then goes to Macumba [voodoo] to ask for a husband."

Because of that mixture, she became possessed, and brought that situation into her life. She opened the door for the enemy to enter. Finally, the sisters found out what was happening, and came to help me. After some time, with much laboring, that lady became free. Glory to God for that! Beloved, be very careful if you are going to seek help in a place that is not the house of God. You are exposing yourself to even greater problems. When you need help, seek it from God, and talk to people who are really prepared to pray for you. Psalm 46:1 says: "God is our refuge and strength, a very present help in trouble" (KJV). Only in Him you will find help for your needs.

9

SERVING AN AWESOME GOD

After I made a firm decision to live for the Lord, I have been used by Jesus in the ministry of His Word. I have taken care of a church as a pastor. I have also worked as a teacher and children's evangelist (three and a half years in my house). I was also president of the women's group, deaconess and was also consecrated as a missionary. I sang in choirs in Brazil as well as in the United States. I even sang in a choir that my son-in-law was the director. I have been used by the mercy of God in the ministry of intercession. I have seen God work in my life greatly. Praise God!

God took care of me when Jefferson left me after 21 years of living together. There were very difficult days of tremendous financial need. Prior to Jefferson, I had become accustomed to having abundant food on the table, a car to drive, and a beach house. After my mistake with Jefferson, I had practically nothing. I returned to work as a sales clerk in a fabric store. However, the pay was very little for the three of us. It was barely enough to pay for the groceries. Jefferson was living with a girl younger than his daughter. He was so involved with her that he completely forgot about his daughters and me. He only cared about satisfying his needs and the wishes of that woman. He once told me, "You're not good enough for me. You are too holy."

One day I was really sad because we were in need of everything at our home. A sister who had the gift of prophecy came to pray for me, and the Lord said, "I am your shepherd; you will lack for nothing." I did like this sister, but I doubted what was said. In my mind, I questioned, "I will lack for nothing?" The person who was the provider of the house was gone. He left no pension and couldn't care less about the needs of the children and me. The suffering and sadness obscured my spiritual vision. I could not see the greatness of this wonderful God and that nothing is impossible for Him.

One night, when I was tired of so many needs, I went to the window to look at the sky, and started talking to God. I like talking to God as a real person. The conversation went something like this: "Lord, I can no longer stand eating sardines". It was the only thing I could buy with my earnings. "I want to eat a steak, but I have no money to buy it. When that man lived here, I ate filet mignon, and now only sardines. I even go to the market when it is time to close in order to buy the leftovers because it is cheaper. I can't stand it anymore!"

When I cried out to God it was already 11:00 p.m., so I went to sleep. When I woke up the next day, one of the sisters from the prayer group that I attended, who really cared for me, called. She lived near my house. "My daughter, have you eaten?" She asked. "No," I answered. "Then come here to my home," she requested. I went pretty fast. Once there, she asked me to extend my arm, and then she put money in my hand. "Take this money. It is for you," she said. Amazed I asked, "Why?" And she explained, "It was Jesus who told me to give you this money in order to buy a steak." "Who told you that I wanted to eat a steak?" I asked. "It was Jesus. He told me to give His servant this money to buy steak," she added.

I was amazed and touched by the care that the Lord had for me. From that day on I was sure that God is alive and real. He sees everything that happens to us and is ready to satisfy the desire of our hearts. I hadn't talked to anyone but Him and then went to sleep. I was amazed by this grand experience of mine. Whenever I can, I tell this testimony to the glory of God. Yet, this was not my only experience like this.

I had another such experience when Celeste was studying Languages and Literature at college. Whenever she had a test, she needed to pay for it. One time she forgot to tell me about her test. Her father had not left any money that day and I had no cash either. If she did not pay the fee, she would have to take the exam on the second round, and consequently, the cost would be higher. In our house with Jefferson, money was always a cause for fights and arguments, so I did everything possible to live in peace. I thought, "I can go to a friend's house and sell a flower arrangement that I have here at home." However, I could not find her, so I offered it to another lady who didn't want it. I returned home sad and downcast thinking, "My God, there will be more fights when that man comes home in the evening."

I was walking looking down at the ground. There was a car parked on my left side. Since I thought I knew the people in the car, I looked down to greet them. I realized that I did not know anyone. However, while getting down to look inside the car, I saw further ahead that there was some crumpled money on the street. I took that money quickly, and went home screaming and celebrating. When I entered my house, I was excited and shouted, "Celeste, look, the money is here. I found it on the street. God is good!" Also, people who owed me money came to pay me that day. Celeste had the money to pay for the test and we still had some leftover.

"Cast your cares on the Lord and he will sustain you;
he will never let the righteous be shaken"
(Psalms 55:22).

When I was working in the U.S. as a nanny for a little boy, I had another unforgettable experience. I spent the week at work and weekends with my family. I remember going to the supermarket where I saw some big, beautiful peaches. It is worth noting that peach is my favorite fruit. They were mouthwatering, but I was short on cash that day. Aside from that, I was saving money, and spending only on main necessities. Despite all that, the desire to eat peaches was great, but I didn't buy them.

Friday came and I went to my daughter's house. We were talking in the kitchen when Celina opened the refrigerator, took out a peach and handed it to me. I said puzzled, "Why are you giving me this peach?" "Mom," she replied, "I was going to eat this peach, but when I was going to put it in my mouth, God told me not to eat it and keep it for you." I looked at her, thanking God for His goodness. I wanted to eat peaches, but because they were so expensive, I didn't buy them. God used my daughter to give me what I wanted to eat. Psalm 37: 4 says, "Take delight in the Lord, and he will give you the desires of your heart". Beloved, there is no doubt God cares about those who belong to him.

> "Look at the birds of the air; they do not sow or reap or store away in barns, and yet your heavenly Father feeds them. Are you not much more valuable than they?" (Matthew 6:26).

10

FREE TO SERVE JESUS

When Jefferson left, I tried to occupy myself with learning more about God. I took a course as a lay preacher. I tried taking a visual communications course, but I didn't do as well because I'm bad at drawing. I studied to be a children's evangelist. I participated in the church choir. I wanted to be busy in the Lord's work. I often went to the deliverance services with my youngest daughter, Celina. Celeste became a believer later. To the glory of God, both now serve the Lord!

Celeste attended the Southern Baptist Seminary in Rio de Janeiro and is a Sunday School teacher. God uses her mightily to minister His Word. She is also certified by the Child Evangelism Fellowship (CEF) and God also uses her to minister to teens. Celina plays acoustic guitar, sings and also ministers the Word in Washington, D.C. where she lives. After Celina went to live in the United States, Celeste married in Brazil to a businessman in the paint sector, and gave me two beautiful granddaughters.

Kate, the older one, is brunette and looks like a model. She is married and lives in Texas, USA. She and her husband have a beautiful baby girl. When she was a child, she was in a magazine cover. She was a part of a children's ministry and led the youth group when she lived in Brazil. Julice, the younger, is also married to a small business owner. She is a very graceful, blonde and was also in a magazine cover. Julice and her husband Gilson gave me great gifts in my three beautiful great-granddaughters.

The year of 1986 was very difficult for me. Celeste was married, my partner had left our home, and I was feeling more and more lonely. Celina, my companion in God's work, was already a young lady. She needed to have friends her age. Since she played and sang, my house was always filled with young people. She was also very beautiful. I had a hard time because of the admirers!

In that year (1986), several American Baptists came to Brazil to evangelize in Rio de Janeiro. It was a great crusade and our church received a delegation from North Carolina. Since there was a shortage of interpreters, my daughter Celina worked as a translator for the American group. The problem was that she didn't have experience translating sermons from the pulpit. But thank God, she did it well.

She became friends with one member of the group, called Paul. He was very playful and everyone loved him. Paul was married but had no children. He so admired my daughter's potential that he decided to pay for her college in North America. When I heard that Celina was willing to go to the United States, to live with a family I had never met, and live in a land whose language I didn't speak, I was terrified.

And what if my daughter would have problems? I wouldn't be able to help her. I could not afford to go get her. I didn't even speak the language. I can say that I fell into a deep despair. I spoke to her father asking him to keep her from traveling. He replied, "Are you crazy? I will not prevent the future of the girl." So I went and asked her pastor, who was a lawyer. He told me, "If you don't allow it, I will sign the permission for the girl to travel." Everyone thought she should go. I didn't want it at all, but this trip was determined by God.

After about four months, Paul came back to my house, now with his wife. They stayed at my house for fifteen days to get to know Celina, our habits and check out my daughter's behavior. They returned with the promise of paying for her studies, taking care of her, and providing her food and shelter. Glory to God they kept their promise! They treated her as if she was their own daughter, and she was able to stay with them until she married an American young man whom she met at college. They paid for everything, including the phone calls she made to me.

My daughter received her Master's Degree in International Trade, and is also a licensed U.S. Customs Broker. Today she is a U.S. citizen, and has lived for twenty-nine years in Washington, D.C. with her husband and two sons, Jonathan and Kevin. I didn't know that God was also preparing my way to go to the United States. Fifteen days before Celina's trip God spoke to a sister, who had the gift of prophecy, to come to my house and talk to me about my daughter's trip. This prophetess belonged to an Assembly of God Church near my house. But she did not know my name or where I lived. She came down the street asking neighbors where the lady lived whose daughter was going to the United States and was very distressed. She asked here and there until someone showed her my house.

When she arrived here, she said, "God sent me here to give you a message. He told me to tell you not to worry about your daughter's trip. It is He who is taking your daughter to that country. She goes like a vessel of honor for God's work, and then you will also go there." After a few years, when my first grandchild, Kevin, was about to be born, I went to the United States. The Lord fulfilled the message that he had sent to me. Since then, I have been living in Brazil and the United States. God has taken care of me in a very special way. I glorify Him for all He has done and still does for me.

11

BABYSITTER IN UNCLE SAM'S LAND

My experience in taking care of children comes from the time I was very young. My first job was as a nanny in Rio de Janeiro. I have lots of practice in childcare. I felt privileged to get a job doing what I loved to do. If you want to be a nanny in the U.S., you need a recommendation. It's a lot of responsibility. There are children that you cannot say "no" to them. We need to be very careful so the child does not get hurt and does not complain about you.

In Washington, D.C., I took care of my own grandchildren and children of others, including Brazilians and Americans. I took care of a girl whose father was a high-ranking military officer at the Pentagon. It was the hardest job I had because neither he nor his wife spoke Portuguese, my native language. But Jesus gave me grace, and I stayed there over a year. When I needed to communicate with them, I used the dictionary or asked my daughter Celina to be my interpreter. The mothers were always calling, wanting to hire me because I knew how to entertain children, I was a Christian, and because it is classy to have a foreign nanny. I taught them little songs about Jesus.

At this job, God gave me a great experience with Him. We were in the summer season of tornadoes. I was playing with the girl when her mother suddenly appeared in the living room. She was fair skinned, but at that moment she was whiter than usual. I asked in English what was happening. She replied, "Tornado." She said that the tornado would pass over our house in fifteen minutes. Tornadoes destroy everything in their way. They pull-up trees, drop houses, and cause great damage. I told her to hold my hand and pray. She understood what I meant. I prayed something like this (I cannot remember precisely because it happened a long time ago), "I rebuke this tornado, and it will not cause any harm in the name of Jesus." We waited because when the tornado passes, it makes a deafening noise. We had to find shelter. However, all was quiet. So I asked: "Where's the tornado?" To which she replied, "I don't know. Looks like it went far from here." Glory to God for the great victory that He gave us that summer afternoon!

I also remember when Celina was pregnant with Kevin. She was in her eighth month of pregnancy. I was there to help when the baby arrived. We were talking and suddenly everything went dark. It was the sign of a great storm. My son-in-law was watching television and said, "Let's go to the basement!" I asked why. He said, "There is a tornado coming through here." I began to be afraid. I took my documents, some blankets and went downstairs, which was the safest place in the house. I just thought that Celina could get nervous, and that could trigger my grandson's premature birth. However, I knew that there is a God who has control of the universe in the palm of His hand, and He has the power to quiet any storm.

I looked for a place from where I could see the sky and cried, "Lord, change the direction of this tornado to a place far away. So that it will not cause any harm to us." As I finished my prayer, I returned to where I was, and I waited. A little later my son-in-law shouted upstairs, "You can come up now! The tornado passed an hour and a half away from here. And where it passed, it caused a lot of damage."

While I was there, I also heard a story of a strong tornado. Its strength was such that it pulled a baby from his mother's arms. Afterwards, this baby was found alive, hooked on a tree. We heard that the child's parents were believers. The enemy often tries to take what belongs to us, and what is ours. However, God cares for us and gives it back. Praise God! Remember Job? He lost his ten children, and all he had. Afterwards, God restored everything to him two-fold.

> "So the Lord blessed the latter end of Job more than his beginning" (Job 42:12a, KJV).

12

EXPERIENCE WITH SNOW

I was in another state taking care of a beautiful blonde girl, the daughter of a Brazilian mother and American father. I often came home on Friday evenings and Monday mornings returned to work. I had to take the subway and go through several stations doing connections. It was Sunday afternoon when the lady called and said: "Come now because I am going to need you tomorrow morning." I was worried because the television and radio were announcing a snow storm for that night.

I told her, "I cannot. Heavy snow will fall today. It is possible that the subway would stop working and that would be dangerous for me to get there." She replied, "Come anyway. I need you here." So I prayed and asked the Lord that during the time that it would take to get to her house no snowflake would fall. And I kept praying. Upon reaching the last station of the subway, her car was already waiting for me. We quickly went home. Arriving there I went into the bedroom and changed my clothes. When I looked out the window, the ground was already all white with snow.

"Wow," I exclaimed. While I was on the way to their home, not even one snowflake fell. Sometimes our faith is weak and we don't believe that our prayer will be heard. Jesus "held" that snow, and protected me until I arrived in safety. Praise God for His protection!

I have had many other experiences with God. On one occasion, I was taking care of two boys. The older was at school, and I had to pick him up at the school bus stop every afternoon. One day a big storm was falling down. It rained all day with a heavy rain, and I had to carry the little boy. The mother called me worried. I could not leave the small child home alone. So I prayed to the Lord.

I asked that the storm would stop so I could pick up the child without problems. Thirty minutes before the boy was supposed to arrive at the bus stop, the storm stopped and the sun came up. When I told their mother what had happened, she was amazed. How could this storm stop exactly at the time the child should arrive? It was God's grace to me. In Psalm 66:19 and 20, it says, "But God has surely listened and has heard my prayer. Praise is to God, who has not rejected my prayer or withheld his love from me!"

I remember the prophet Elijah; he was a man subject to passions as we are. He was annoyed by what King Ahab was doing. He said, "As the Lord, the God of Israel, lives, whom

I serve, there will be neither dew nor rain in the next few years except at my word" (I Kings 17:13). God heard the word of Elijah, and Israel suffered a severe drought. The word of the person who fears God has much power.

You must be wondering why I changed jobs so much. As I don't speak fluent English, I took care of children who were still small. When they were older, parents preferred to put them in a daycare or kindergarten where there were many activities for young children. They were learning to speak, and needed to learn their native language. I was in another house near the home of my daughter Celina. In this job, I took care of a beautiful little boy. He was very sweet. I really loved all the children that God allowed me to care for over the years. When I had to go, I left them crying. I still have pictures of almost all of them.

Celina and I had the habit of praying through the telephone. I was praying through my cell phone with her when suddenly it blacked out. I thought I needed to charge the battery, but this was not the problem. So I said I was not going to spend money repairing that phone. Later, I checked and it was still off. I woke up at dawn and prayed for my cell phone. The next day in the afternoon it was working again. This happened to the honor and glory of the Lord.

I always returned home on weekends to be with my family. Kevin, my grandson, asked to sleep next to me and, of course, I let him. One night, when everyone was asleep, at about one o'clock in the morning, Kevin started to cough. He could not stop coughing. There was nothing I could do. He is fair skinned, but there was a moment he looked at me all red and sweaty. I thought, "Lord, what can I do?" So I cried out to the God of heaven, and immediately, that cough went away. Another time, God healed my son-in-law, Celina's husband, from an allergy that left his arms and stomach raw. He couldn't even put on his clothes. In this experience, Celina prayed with me.

Our family traveled to Brazil for vacation. We rented a house because there were many us. We were getting ready to visit some friends. My daughter was giving Jonathan a bath. Suddenly, I heard screams. I found my daughter stunned, and my son-in-law as white as snow, speechless. My grandson had fallen, and he had a deep cut on his head above the neck. When I saw that scene, I ran and put my hand over the cut. I prayed and the bleeding stopped. Soon the boy was running around and getting into mischief again. We didn't have to go to the emergency room. In fact, we were staying in a remote part of the city without immediate access to medical help. Jesus healed him. Hallelujah! Glory to God for His goodness!

Jesus has been faithful in my life. When I look back and see from where Jesus brought me out, I just want to glorify Him for all that He has done for me. I have traveled alone to the United States and Brazil in airplanes. This really is a miracle considering that I suffered with panic disorder.

13

MY FIRST JOB IN D.C.

Eventually, my grandson no longer needed my care, so I decided to look for work. In the United States, especially in Washington DC, life is very expensive. Besides, I didn't want to depend on my daughter financially. While talking with my daughter, we decided to put an ad in the church bulletin offering my nanny services, since I can do it well, given my experience. It is common to post ads in evangelical churches for seeking work.

A couple of pastors of a big church saw my ad and invited me to an interview. This family was upper middle class. They lived in a high-class neighborhood in the city. They had lived some time in Brazil and adopted two Brazilian children. A girl and a boy who were almost teenagers. The family wanted a person who could speak Portuguese with them. I was kind of a tutor, just so they wouldn't lose touch with their native language. They loved Brazil and Brazilians as well. I was worried about taking a position as a tutor. However, my certification from CEF helped me a lot. Anyway, they liked me and I liked them. So, I was hired.

My work in the house consisted more of speaking Portuguese, organizing the menu and seeing what needed to be done. The house had three floors and with the mess the boys made there was a lot to organize. They had four children, two adopted and two biological. The two biological children were young men who attended college away from home. They only came home on holidays, the day of Thanksgiving or Christmas. The hostess, Sara, became my friend, and I often sat on the edge of her bed to hear her share her heart as well as to comfort her. Fortunately, she spoke and understood my Portuguese.

Sara was a woman of great class. She always put together events to raise funds for the church's functions. And during these events, she invited the American high society, offering elegant dinners. Imagine who she invited to sit at the President's table: me. She insisted that I sit with them or beside her brother, who was divorced. Louis was very nice to me. And occasionally, he showed up at the house with the excuse of having a cup of coffee or to learn a word in Portuguese.

I remember once when Sara hired a chef to make French food. She told me, "You will go to this dinner!" I let her go ahead, and I promptly locked myself in my room. She searched for me during dinner, but didn't see me. So, she came home to get me. After we got there, she introduced me to many important people. I just said, "Nice to meet you." I felt like a fish out of water in the middle of those stylish people. I can say that I didn't eat anything at that dinner. I passed everything to Louis. He was enjoying it because as they served me, then I gave it to him. I only ate French bread and salad that day. When I came home, I got a snack because I was hungry!

Sara loved me, and I loved her too. Sara was very special to me. When I fell down the stairs because I slipped, breaking a rib (I just found out I had broken my rib a month later when I went to the doctor), she hired a maid to do the job, and didn't want me to do anything. Thank God, Jesus healed me from this broken rib.

While my mother was alive, I did not want to be a resident in this country. So, I spent six months in the USA and one year in Brazil. After God called her home, I decided to become a U.S. resident. I am currently living in Texas, in the city of San Antonio and I attend a Hispanic Baptist church. Whenever I can, I go to Washington to see old friends who live there.

Beloved, I said that I frequented places of the highest class; but for me, it didn't change my way of being simple. And I want to stay simple, not aspiring to great things. Often, blessings come to my hands without me looking for them. I like the text of Matthew 16: 26, 27 that says, "What good will it be for someone to gain the whole world, yet forfeit their soul? Or what can anyone give in exchange for their soul? For the Son of Man is going to come in his Father's glory with his angels, and then he will reward each person according to what they have done." The reward of God is our greatest treasure.

Thank you, Lord for everything you have done for me!

14

TITHES & OFFERINGS

I am grateful to God for the miracles he has worked in my life. I am grateful for His provision because he has supported me in all my needs. He has given more than I have asked or thought. Today, because of Jesus, I have clothes and shoes to give to those in need. I always make donations because sometimes I need to make space, and also because people give me many things. The time when I had no clothes to wear is behind me. Praise the Lord!

Since I committed myself to the Lord, Jesus turned my heart to be a faithful tither and give offerings to His work. Whenever I can, I help the brethren who are in need. The saying "it is in giving that one receives" has been fulfilled in my life. I don't do it with the intention of receiving something in return. The blessing of sharing is within me.

Maybe, because I had so much need in the past, now I have abundance. I see so many needy people! This moves me.

It is more blessed to give than to receive (Acts 20:35). So, whenever you can, offer something. Be generous. Offer a word of encouragement to someone who is discouraged. Offer a smile. Offer a heartfelt hug. Take hope to someone who is afflicted. Tell them that Jesus loves them. Offer forgiveness. You will see how you will feel light.

I'd like to tell you my experience with forgiveness. It happened with my husband's mistress. Through him, I found out she was very angry with me. I hadn't done anything to her, but she hated me. This person caused me great harm by destroying my family. However, Jesus told me to go to her, and ask her for forgiveness. I said, "Jesus, I won't go! She is the one who has to ask me for forgiveness." However, the Lord ordered me, "Go and ask her for forgiveness!" Obediently, I went, and asked if she had anything against me. She said yes, because of a word I had said about her years ago. Then, I asked her to forgive me, and that it was not my intention to offend her. Then, I gave her a big hug. Her face shone and I left there feeling really light, free.

EPILOGUE

Before I finish this story, I want to share with you a little bit more of my journey. I was in San Antonio when Jefferson called me. He said, "When will you come to Brazil?" I replied: "Soon. Why?" "I need to talk about us," he said. He wanted to talk about us?! After thirty years apart? I wondered, "My God, what could this man want?" It had been over ten years that he was alone, and by alone, I mean he wasn't living with anyone.

He said to me, "Let's work on a document stating we have a stable union so you can have the right to my things. You are the only person who deserves to share my inheritance." I told him: "I don't know what this is, but I will pray." I said goodbye to him and went to pray, and find out what was he was proposing to me.

I went to Brazil and learned that stable unions are for people who live together, but are not married. They sign a document proving that they are together. If one of the partners dies, the survivor would have the same rights as those who are legally married. Amazingly, my telephone bills were mailed to his house. I was in Brazil, when he called saying, "I'm going there to give you the phone bill they sent to my house. I don't know why they sent your phone bill over here." When he arrived, I told him, "I cannot do this. This stable union is not right for me. I haven't lived with you for over thirty years."

Then he spoke, "But we've already lived together, and we have two daughters." I said, "But at this moment we don't live together anymore. If I do that, I would be lying. I am God's servant. I will not lie." And I kept praying. Everyone I talked to said that stable unions were fine, but I didn't feel at peace. I talked with a lawyer friend of mine, and she said, "If he wants to do it, why don't you get married?"

I went back to pray, now saying, "Lord God, if you want this to happen, I'll talk to him about us getting married. And if he accepts, it is your will." Again, a phone bill went to his house for the second time. When he came to bring the bill, I said to him, "Why don't we get married?" He kept quiet, and smirked as he left. Celeste said: "He will never agree to get married."

Fifteen days after I made the proposal, he agreed on getting married. The enemy fought until the end to hinder our wedding. We began to process the paperwork, and we needed two witnesses. We arrived before the clerk who takes care of the documentation. Everything checked out in my case. When it was Jefferson's turn, the lady said, "This is not your document; it belongs to someone else." He had taken the birth certificate of his son. Then, he went back home to look for the right papers. I went home to wait for him so we could go together to the courthouse. Then, one of the witnesses called and said that he couldn't wait for Jefferson because he had to go to work in the afternoon.

I literally was pulling my hair out! Where would I find another witness in 30 minutes, before the courthouse would close, and who had all their needed documents and identification. I started calling a lot of people, and they would say: "What? Who is getting married?" I would answer, "It's me, I can explain afterwards. There is no time to explain right now." At last, I got the witness I needed and we set a date and time for the ceremony. I arrived first and then one of the witnesses had to leave for a job interview and couldn't come. Once again, I was looking for someone at the last minute to be my witness for the wedding.

Since I couldn't find anybody, my daughter Celeste offered to do it, and we left for the courthouse to celebrate the wedding of Mr. Jefferson and Ms. Mira. We arrived there, and when it was time to see the judge, the master of ceremony said, "Mr. Jefferson, you cannot get married like this, dressed in shorts." So, I stayed there with the guests, and Celeste went with him to purchase pants so he could get married. It seems funny, but it was really hard for me to face this situation at the courthouse after all I had been through. Someone said that somebody should go with him because he could, perhaps, leave the bride waiting... At the end, he was able to find the pants, and no longer had any excuses. Thank God, all went well, and one more time God gave me the victory!

Now I understand why God didn't let any other man like me. It was because He wanted us to correct a situation that was pending in our past. That is why I love this God. He is faithful and takes care of His people. When He determines a blessing, no one can stop it. He does nothing halfway and always completes the work He begins. In every way, Jesus gave me a second chance. He wants to do the same for you.

ABOUT THE AUTHOR

MISSIONARY MIRA SOUSA currently lives in Rio de Janeiro, Brazil. She frequently visits the United States. As a member of the Baptist Church, she does social work with the local community in the clothing ministry.

She is a member of the church "Jesus Christ is Life." She taught the Bible in Sunday school and served as a minister and preacher of the Gospel. She is certified by CEF—Child Evangelism Fellowship in Brazil and held a children's evangelism class at her home for over three years. She also served as a pastor at Mercy Christian Church for three and half years. She is married, has two daughters, four grandchildren and four great-grandchildren.

Sister Mira wrote this book not only to honor and glorify her God, but also to give her testimony and encourage people. Finally, the intent is to also show you, the reader, the impact that prayer can have in your life.

Please read Joshua 10:12-14.

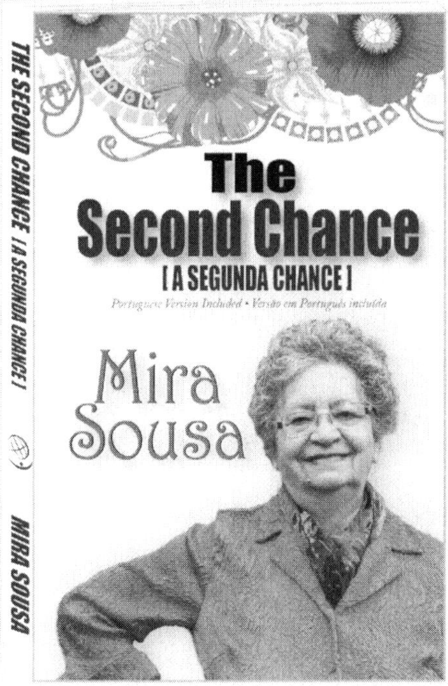

In THE SECOND CHANCE, Missionary Mira Sousa shares her life journey which begins as a poor young girl in Brazil. Her life was full of poverty and heartaches where she felt no one in the world cared about her until she came to a saving grace in the Lord Jesus Christ. Mira found out she was not alone and through her faith in God, she would overcome in this life. Prayer—her connection with God—has been her mainstay. Learn about the love of God and the power of prayer through this inspirational story.

ISBN: 978-1-60273-092-2 • Bilingual edition: English & Portuguese

Parsons Publishing House

Your Voice Your World™

Available at your local
bookstore or order online at www.Amazon.com

CAPTURING THE HEART OF GOD
by Diane Parsons
God created man for His good pleasure. Our most satisfying goal should be to bring delight to our heavenly Father. Make it your goal today to do those things which please God. This book contains practical tips on capturing God's heart and becoming His delight everyday.
ISBN: 9781602730182 • 140 pages • $10.95 USD.

NEXT LEVEL: RAISING THE STANDARD OF GRACE
by Pastor Robert Gay
In this book, Robert is sounding a trumpet call from heaven, engaging the reader to see the Ten Commandments afresh from the empowering view of God's Grace. Robert clearly and biblically explains how Grace empowers us to live godly, holy lives above sin. There is no limit to the success, prosperity, and blessings that will surround you when you apply these principles.
ISBN: 9781602730427 • 216 pages • $14.95 USD.

INFUSE—ACTIVATING HEAVEN ON EARTH
by Dr. Kevin Bordeaux
This book will guide you in your understanding of how to have a living, dynamic relationship with God and then spread that relationship to the world. Jesus told us to pray, "On earth as it is in heaven." To do this, we must know what is happening in heaven. The Book of Revelation is not only a futuristic, apocalyptic account, but a glimpse into heaven. It is also a glimpse into how our lives can be funnels where the world can experience heaven daily through us. ISBN: 9781602730113 • 138 pages • $12.95 USD.

EMERGING AS AN INNOVATIVE CHRISTIAN LEADER

by Dr. Darrell Parsons

Ideas become the catalyst for change, and change becomes the catalyst for innovation. Innovation is centered on creating or enhancing value. With this understanding, Darrell Parsons articulates twelve of the most important competencies which are imperative for today's innovative leader. When dealing with any group, from families to organizations, emerging leaders can begin the process of innovative leadership development by working on the common core competencies identified in this book.

ISBN: 9781602730656 • 228 pages • $12.95 USD.

WHY DO I DO THE THINGS I DO?

Understanding Personalities by Dr. Darrell Parsons

In this insightful book, Darrell Parsons identifies the four primary types of personalities and how they interact together. As you grow in understanding, you will gain the tools you need for developing successful relationships in all areas of your life.

ISBN: 9781602730199 • 132 pages • $10.95 USD.

RELEASE YOUR WORDS—IMPACT YOUR WORLD

by Dr. Darrell Parsons

Your words can make a difference! God has placed treasures inside you; learn to release them to influence your world. In this book, Darrell Parsons challenges you to use your voice to impact the world around you today.

ISBN: 9781602730007 • 140 pages • $9.95 USD.

SONSHIP: THE MANTLE. THE JOURNEY. THE DOUBLE-PORTION

by Pastor Joshua Gay

In this book, Robert is sounding a trumpet call from heaven, engaging the reader to see the Ten Commandments afresh from the empowering view of God's grace. Robert clearly and biblically explains how grace empowers us to live godly, holy lives above sin. There is no limit to the success, prosperity, and blessings that will surround you when you apply these principles.

ISBN: 9781602730526 • 180 pages • $12.95 USD.

JESUS IN 3D
by Pastor Robert Gay
Every dimension of the ministry of Jesus is critical for us to have ultimate effectiveness for the kingdom of God. Today, if you want to reflect the life of God, you must receive and activate all that He did, everything He said, and everything He demonstrated. Learn how God's grace actually empowers your life to be blessed as you shine as a reflection of Jesus in the earth.
ISBN: 9781602730588• 102 pages • $9.95 USD.

FAITH AFTER FAILURE
by Dr. Sandie Freed
In this book, you will discover about the times when we find ourselves in the pit of despair and are then equipped by God's grace to move forward once again and experience complete fulfillment in Christ. There is no mission impossible for God. "Mission Possible" awaits you as you read ***Faith After Failure: Reconnecting With Your Destiny.***
ISBN: 9781602730557 • 208 pages • $13.95 USD.

upRIGHTING RELATIONSHIPS
by Linda Roeder
This book by Linda Roeder is filled with wisdom, hope, and practical help for your relationships. Based on biblical principles, this nitty-gritty book encourages you to grow closer to God and others as you learn about His love. Whether a relationship is strong and growing or difficult and unresolved, you can learn to please God and be at peace.
ISBN: 9781602730755 • 174 pages • $12.95 USD.

SONSHIP: THE MANTLE. THE JOURNEY. THE DOUBLE-PORTION
by Pastor Robert Gay
In this timely book, veteran author and pastor, Robert Gay, clearly articulates God's practical and spiritual plans to build healthy and growing churches. Both pastors and congregations will be equipped to rise to the challenge as this compelling revelation is released. You will find the answers to your ministry questions contained in this one masterful text.
ISBN: 9781602730892 • 224 pages • $14.95 USD.

The Second Chance

[A SEGUNDA CHANCE]

Portuguese Version Included • Versão em Português incluída

Mira Sousa

Parsons Publishing House
Christiansburg, Virginia USA

DEDICATÓRIA

Àquele que sempre dá uma segunda chance: Deus.

MEUS SINCEROS AGRADECIMENTOS

Ao Senhor Jesus Cristo. Meu verdadeiro amigo—fiel nas batalhas.
A minha família. Que tem sido minha fonte de inspiração.
A minha amada Igreja Jesus Cristo é a Vida, que tanto tem me apoiado nas horas difíceis.
As irmãs do círculo de oração aqui do Brasil e às do círculo de oração Lírio dos Vales, nos Estados Unidos. Que tem me sustentado com seu carinho e seu amoroso cuidado.
A Selma Alves, que me deu forças com sua preciosa oração através do telefone.
A Célia Feldpausch, por seu incentivo e orações preciosas.
A querida irmã Quézia, que cuidou da digitação desta obra.
A família Parsons, que cuidou da publicação desta obra.

A minha gratidão.
Missionária Mira Sousa

ÍNDICE

PREFÁCIO

Quando cheguei para morar em meu prédio, no ano de 2009, ouvi falar de uma irmã que fez um lindo trabalho com as crianças em sua casa. Mas, agora morava nos Estados Unidos. Um tempo depois conheci a irmã Mira em uma de suas visitas ao Brasil.

Minha primeira impressão foi de uma pessoa muito simples. Ao ouvi-la pregar, percebi que ali estava uma serva de Deus que realmente conhecia seu Senhor.

Só conheci mais detalhes de sua vida quando fui convidada a digitar o manuscrito deste livro. Nele a autora nos apresenta um Deus pessoal e íntimo daqueles que O buscam. E não o Deus distante e indiferente que muitos reverenciam.

Em todo o livro ela faz questão de frisar como Deus é bom e misericordioso. Seu coração grato nos leva a dar glórias a esse Deus maravilhoso em todo o tempo da narrativa.

Não há uma apologia à prosperidade, ao ter bens materiais, mas com muita simplicidade, ela conta como Deus supriu todas as suas necessidades espirituais, materiais e emocionais. Aliás, basta conhecer a irmã Mira pessoalmente para ver que ela não ostenta riquezas. Mas, também deixa claro que o nosso Deus tem prazer em abençoar e cumprir Sua Palavra que diz que o justo não mendigará o pão. Tudo isso para que o nome do Senhor seja glorificado. Não por sermos bons, mas sim porque Ele é bom para conosco.

A Segunda Chance também nos ensina que antes de qualquer coisa, necessitamos de salvação. Precisamos reconhecer que somos pecadores e Jesus é o único que pode nos salvar da condenação eterna. Não o Jesus feito por mãos de homens que muitos insistem em adorar, em sua cegueira espiritual. Mas, sim o verdadeiro Jesus que veio ao mundo, morreu, ressuscitou e vive.

Enfim, cada experiência descrita neste livro é um testemunho vivo que vai encher o coração do leitor de esperança em Jesus. Vai fazer a fé crescer e a certeza de que "Deus está vendo tudo o que você está passando, nada está oculto aos Seus olhos. E no momento certo, Ele virá com o socorro e o livramento que você precisa" (Mira Sousa).

—Quézia Soares da Silva
Fonoaudiologa

INTRODUÇÃO

"Bendize ó minha alma ao Senhor e tudo que há em mim bendiga o seu santo nome. Bendize, ó minha alma ao Senhor e não te esqueças de nenhum de seus benefícios (Salmo 103:1-2).

Quando Deus se revelou a mim através de respostas de orações eu senti o desejo de escrever um livro que levasse as pessoas a saberem que Deus existe, é real e cuida do seu povo.

Você meu irmão em Cristo, que está lendo este livro, saiba: Deus está vendo tudo o que está passando; nada está oculto aos Seus olhos. No momento certo Ele virá com o socorro e livramento que você precisa.

A confirmação para eu escrever este livro veio muitos anos depois. Quando Deus tem um plano na nossa vida, pode demorar, mas um dia o que Deus determinou pra você, se cumprirá.

Em maio de 2010 eu já estava morando nos Estados Unidos e estávamos numa nova igreja, por sinal, muito avivada. Tínhamos encontrado novos irmãos. A [1]koinonia era muito boa. Como eu ia fazer aniversário nesse mês, pedi à minha filha Celina uma festa com um culto de ação de graças. Queria agradecer a Deus. Ela convidou alguns amigos, dentre eles o casal Darrell e Diane. Darrell era da aeronáutica. Ele e sua esposa são donos de editora. Mas, eu não sabia desses detalhes. Diane só fala Inglês e eu Português. Nossa comunicação era pequena. Enfim, Deus havia preparado tudo. Ninguém, exceto Deus, conhecia meu desejo de escrever um livro. Eu o guardei no meu coração.

Terminado o culto, Darrell me perguntou, "Posso orar por você?" Eu disse que sim. Ele orou em Inglês e minha filha, claro, foi a interprete.

Depois Diane orou e disse, "Eu tenho um recado de Deus pra você. Quer ouvir?" Quando respondi que sim, ela começou a dizer, "Deus tem te dado algo. Ele quer que você compartilhe isso com as pessoas. Ele quer que você escreva um livro. Eu vou publicar esse livro na língua que você quiser".

Eu fiquei parada. Ou melhor, fiquei maravilhada porque o desejo do meu coração estava sendo confirmado pelo Senhor, através da Diane. Foi o meu grande presente de aniversário. Há muitos anos eu sentia o desejo de colocar no papel e fazer conhecido o que Deus fez em minha vida. O que vivi ao longo da minha caminhada com Ele, quando eu O conheci de verdade. Eu pensava, "Como vou escrever um livro? Já não sou jovem, nem sou graduada em nenhuma universidade. Sou estrangeira aqui neste país (estava morando nos Estados Unidos da América). Quem vai querer saber da minha história?" E com tantas perguntas eu estava esquecendo que é Deus quem capacita. Não devemos olhar para nossa incapacidade porque quando Deus escolhe alguém para fazer algo para Sua obra, Ele capacita e dá as ferramentas.

Confesso que levei muito tempo para decidir a contar minha trajetória de vida cristã.

> Não temas ó Sião, não se enfraqueçam as tuas mãos. O Senhor teu Deus está no meio de ti, poderoso para te salvar; Ele se deleitará em ti com alegria; calar-se-á por seu amor; regozijar-se-á em ti com júbilo (Sofonias 3:16-17).

Esse era o desejo do meu coração. Fazer conhecido o que Deus havia feito por mim. E que o nome Dele fosse glorificado.

E se Ele fez por mim pode fazer também por você.

Eu me achava muito simples para escrever um livro. Eu dava todo tipo de desculpas, assim como fez Moisés quando foi chamado por Deus para tirar o povo do Egito. Para levá-los à terra de Canaã, a terra prometida.

> Então disse Moisés ao Senhor: Ah, Senhor, eu não sou homem eloquente nem de ontem, nem

> de anteontem, nem ainda desde que tens falado ao teu servo; porque sou pesado de boca e pesado de língua. E disse o Senhor: quem fez a boca do homem? Ou quem fez o mudo ou o surdo, ou o que vê, ou o cego? Não sou eu o Senhor? (Êxodo 4: 10-11).

Diante de tantas desculpas comecei a escrever.

Nasce uma escritora que achava que não tinha capacidade para escrever sua história. Eu achava que escrever um livro era como abater um gigante. Porém, a pedra foi certeira na cabeça do gigante. E aqui estou eu contando a história da minha vida.

[1]A palavra *koinonia* é muito usada no meio evangélico para designar comunhão.

1

MINHA FAMÍLIA DE MATUTOS

Nasci na década de 40, no Rio Grande do Norte—Brasil, numa cidade chamada Itabaiana, no meio do mato.

Não tínhamos luz elétrica nem transporte para irmos às cidades mais próximas—Itaipu e Baixa Verde. Os meios de locomoção eram o lombo de cavalo, jumento ou na carroceria de caminhão. O caminhão passava uma vez por semana, sempre aos sábados pela manhã. Pegava os passageiros de manhã e trazia de volta à tarde. Os passageiros passavam o dia na cidade onde vendiam seus produtos na feira, que tinha de tudo: cereais, rapadura, queijo, frango e até comida. Lembro-me que ficávamos na expectativa da volta do papai trazendo doces e alguma coisa para comermos.

Lembro-me bem de meu pai com seu chapéu de palha e minha mãe com o cabelo preso atrás da cabeça feito um coque e seus vestidos de chitão com aquelas flores bem grandes. Minha mãe tinha um rosto suave. Era muito mansa, mas quando ficava brava eu saía de perto correndo.

Minha família era composta por quatro pessoas: meu pai, minha mãe, minha irmã Dora, sempre muito tímida, e eu. Dora era a preferida do papai por ser a filha mais velha.

Dora tinha uma particularidade: sempre que chegava uma visita para comer ela corria e se escondia atrás da casa. Não gostava de comer na frente de ninguém. Hoje, aos 78 anos ainda não gosta de comer conosco.

Nossa casa era muito pobre. Era feita de barro e coberta de telha. Não tinha moveis na sala, nem cama no quarto, ou melhor, tinha um estrado de madeira que meu pai colocava um cobertor em cima para eles dormirem.

Na sala tinha apenas um banco de madeira onde meu pai fazia suas cestas. O fogão era à lenha, as panelas de barro e eu e minha irmã dormíamos em redes, como é o costume dos nordestinos. Uma noite acordei com uma cobra enrolada no punho de minha rede. Felizmente, não era cobra venenosa. Que susto!

Meu pai era lavrador. Trabalhava na roça. Plantava para comer. Mas, como meu pai não gostava do serviço pesado, nós passávamos muitas dificuldades. Nossa colheita mal dava para nos alimentar. Eu era magra e anêmica.

Não tinha leite para as crianças, a carne era dos frangos que se criava, a farinha era feita em casa e para o café da manhã tinha batata doce ou abóbora cozida, amassada com leite de coco. Não se usava óleo para fazer comida. Não havia mesa em minha casa. Mamãe colocava um pano no chão e sentávamos em volta para comer. A luz vinha da lamparina a querosene ou de lampião, uma espécie de abajur de vidro.

Eu só tinha um vestido que estava rasgado na altura da barriga. Ficava tentando amarrar os fiapos de cima aos de baixo para fechar o buraco. Não sei por que minha mãe não costurava. Ela parecia infeliz e deprimida com aquela situação de pobreza. Quando eu tomava banho ficava enrolada num lençol, esperando a roupa secar. Nessa época, tive febre tifóide e meus cabelos caíram totalmente. Graças a Deus não me deixou sequela.

Meu pai era um homem rude e cheio de manias. Quando mamãe lhe dava o café, ele sempre olhava para dentro da xícara, para ver o reflexo do seu rosto ali. Caso não visse, não bebia o café.

Eu e minha irmã Dora não tínhamos brinquedos. Como eu gostava de brincar de fazer comida, todas as vezes que mamãe matava um frango, separava os miúdos para eu cozinhar. Minhas panelas eram latas de carne em conserva que ela guardava pra mim. Eu sempre gostei de cozinhar. Até hoje dizem que cozinho muito bem.

Meu pai era como dizem no Nordeste, aluado—um dia estava bem, no outro emburrado. Creio que era bipolar. Quando estava feliz, tocava um instrumento que ele mesmo fez, parecido com um berimbau. Minha irmã o acompanhava com seu pandeiro feito de lata de goiabada. Sentávamos na frente de casa e nos divertíamos muito.

Quando eu falei pro meu neto Jonathan, de dez anos, que não tinha brinquedos quando criança, ele foi até o seu quarto, pegou um dos seus brinquedos e disse, "Olha aqui, vovó, esses são pra você brincar, ok? Depois você me devolve."

Nossa religião era católica, mas não me lembro de ter assistido uma missa sequer nos meus tempos de criança. Porém, rezávamos em casa, conhecíamos todos os "santos": coração de Jesus, nossa senhora, são Severino do Ramo, frei Damião e padre Cícero Romão. Tínhamos algumas fotos de santos em nossa parede. Era o costume por lá. O sonho do nordestino era ir ao Ceará visitar o padre Cícero Romão Batista. Os católicos acreditam até hoje que esse padre faz milagres. Era muita ignorância espiritual. Como poderia um morto fazer alguma coisa?

Em Eclesiastes 9:5 lemos:

> Porque os vivos sabem que hão de morrer, mas os mortos não sabem coisa nenhuma; nem tão pouco eles tem jamais recompensa, mas a sua memória ficou entregue ao esquecimento.

2

VISITA DA TIA

Quando eu tinha cinco anos de idade veio nos visitar uma tia que morava na capital do Rio Grande do Norte, Natal. Tia Maria era o seu nome. Lembro-me como se fosse hoje. Era uma senhora simpática de rosto redondo, cabelos pretos amarrados como um coque atrás, olhos negros redondos, sobrancelhas grossas e um largo sorriso bondoso. Ela usava um vestido simples e de mangas compridas; era crente de uma denominação pentecostal. Essa tia me apresentou Jesus, o Salvador.

Eu amava Jesus, porém o Jesus que eu conhecia era de barro e de madeira. Estava morto na cruz com uma coroa de espinhos na cabeça e não podia fazer nada por ninguém.

> Tem boca, mas não falam; tem olhos, mas não veem. Tem ouvidos, mas não ouvem; nariz tem, mas não cheiram; tem mãos, mas não apalpam; tem pés, mas não andam; nem som algum sai de sua garganta. Tornem-se semelhantes a eles os que os fazem e todos que neles confiam (Salmo 115:5-8).

Como eu não conhecia o Deus vivo, estava nessa condição sem vida, adorando um Deus que nada podia fazer por mim. Glórias a Deus que enviou a minha tia para me apresentar o Deus vivo e poderoso, real e verdadeiro, que pode me ajudar em qualquer dificuldade que eu tenha que passar. Porém, levou um longo tempo para eu conhecer de verdade esse Deus vivo e ter experiências com Ele.

Minha tia me disse que aquele Jesus que eu via era de madeira, mas existia um que era real. Eu guardei no meu coração de criança as palavras dela. Nunca perca a oportunidade de apresentar o Senhor Jesus para as pessoas, contar do Seu amor por nós.

Eu morava na roça. Lá não havia nenhuma igreja evangélica para eu frequentar. Além disso, falavam muitas coisas contra os crentes. Contavam coisas mentirosas sobre os evangélicos. Espalharam uma história que enquanto os crentes ficavam ajoelhados orando, um "Jesus" de rabo passeava no meio deles. Não sei de onde surgiu o boato. Só pode ser coisa do nosso inimigo.

Eu não me preocupei com isso. Guardei o que me foi dito. A semente do evangelho foi plantada em meu coração e ficou ali até germinar e dar seus frutos para a glória de Deus.

Meus pais nunca souberam que minha tia falou de sua fé em Jesus para mim. Eu ouvia as pessoas dizerem: "Esses crentes, esses bodes!" Havia muito preconceito e perseguição. Graças a Deus, hoje no Brasil o evangelho tem melhor aceitação.

3

DA ROÇA PRA CIDADE GRANDE

Quando eu tinha sete para oito anos minha mãe ficou muito doente e nosso pai colocou uma sobrinha dele em casa para cuidar de nós. Com o passar do tempo ele teve um caso amoroso com essa sobrinha e foi embora, viver com ela.

Meu tio, irmão da minha mãe, sabendo da nossa difícil situação nos levou para Natal onde ele vivia. E fomos morar, então, com meus avós maternos.

A doença de minha mãe deixou sequela: encurtou uma de suas pernas. Ela passou a andar com dificuldade, mancando. Nosso tio nos ajudava com as despesas da casa e com vestuário. Quando aparecia alguém precisando de doméstica, minha mãe ia trabalhar para ajudar nas despesas. Ela gostava de fazer cocadas e bolos para vender. Como nossa renda era pouca, aos nove anos de idade, fui trabalhar como doméstica também.

Quando minha mãe me deixou na casa da família, onde iria trabalhar, chorei muito. Porque não queria ficar longe dela. Aos finais de semana ela me buscava. E assim foi minha infância, cheia de necessidades. E sem saber o que é ser criança, brincar sem ter preocupação de não ter o que comer.

Minha irmã Dora se casou aos dezessete anos, porém seu esposo ganhava pouco e não podia nos ajudar. Nessa época meu avô faleceu. Minha mãe havia conseguido um trabalho de doméstica e eu fui morar só com minha avó materna. Juntas frequentávamos uma igreja pentecostal muito rigorosa. Era daquelas igrejas que não podia cortar cabelo, usar batom, brinco ou qualquer tipo de vaidade. Nem sequer podia usar desodorante. Os vestidos tinham que ser de manga comprida. Imagine isso no Nordeste onde faz muito calor a maior parte do ano. Era bastante desconfortável!

Eu já era uma adolescente. Estava começando a paquerar. Meu tio, que era muito cuidadoso comigo achou que minha avó não podia mais tomar conta de mim. Então me entregou pra minha mãe.

Eu não tinha onde morar e nós duas ficávamos na casa de parentes. A cada semana íamos para uma casa diferente, não tínhamos lugar fixo. Parecíamos uma bola de pingue-pongue. Eu detestava aquilo. Desejava ardentemente ter minha casa, um canto só meu, onde eu pudesse ter privacidade.

Pensava em me casar, mas eu era muito jovem ainda. Achava que se me casasse, tudo ia ficar bem. Mais tarde descobri que não era nada disso.

É bom casarmos e termos casa própria, mas a felicidade verdadeira, só está em Jesus Cristo, quando nos abrigamos à sombra de Suas asas.

"Ele te cobrirá com as suas penas e debaixo das suas asas estarás seguro. Ele me invocará, e eu lhe responderei; estarei com ele na angústia; livrá-lo-ei e o glorificarei" (Salmo 91:4 e 15).

4

O ENGANO DO MUNDO E SUA FALSA ALEGRIA

Quando fiz dezesseis anos minha mãe conseguiu alugar um local para morarmos. Mamãe ainda não era convertida. Só conheceu Jesus na velhice. E eu não tinha o suporte de uma igreja e dos irmãos. Saí dos caminhos do Senhor e passei trinta anos fora da casa do Pai. Afastei-me completamente, saindo da presença de Deus.

Não sabia que esse passo que havia dado por causa da vaidade, por querer "aproveitar" a vida iria mais tarde me custar muito caro.

A Palavra de Deus diz em Mateus 12:43-45:

> E quando o espírito imundo tem saído do homem anda por lugares áridos buscando repouso e não o encontrando diz: Voltarei para

> minha casa donde sai. E voltando acha-a desocupada, varrida e adornada. Então vai e leva consigo outros sete espíritos piores do que ele, e entrando habitam ali e são os últimos atos desse homem piores que o primeiro.

Foi o que aconteceu comigo. Comecei a consultar horóscopos, fui à cartomantes, aos terreiros de macumba. Dançava nos clubes famosos e quando chegava o carnaval me entregava à folia nos trios elétricos. Participei de concurso de beleza e ganhei em segundo lugar. Sentia que tinha o mundo aos meus pés.

Recordo de uma vez que estava num clube—não era um lugar de boa fama para uma jovem de família, mas estava na rebeldia. Quando as amigas me convidavam, eu ia para qualquer lugar com elas. Nesse dia, já passava de uma e meia da manhã e eu num lugar como aquele. Ninguém se preocupava comigo. Digo ninguém na terra, mas meu Pai do Céu estava me vendo e falou comigo claramente naquele lugar.

Ouvi uma voz dizer dentro de mim: "O que você está fazendo aqui? Esse não é lugar pra você". Imediatamente peguei minha bolsa e fui embora pra casa sozinha, mesmo sendo de madrugada. Eu achava que ninguém se preocupava comigo, porém há um versículo na Bíblia que diz:

> Pode uma mulher esquecer-se tanto de seu filho que cria, que se não compadeça dele, do filho do seu ventre? Mas ainda que esta se esquecesse, eu, todavia, me não esquecerei de ti (Isaías 49:15).

5

DEUS CUIDOU DE MIM

Nesses tempos modernos ninguém tem paciência, nem tempo a perder com os outros. Nem mesmo consigo. Na era da informática, micro-ondas, tudo é feito muito rápido. Não se separa tempo para orar, para estar a sós com Deus, ouvir o que Ele tem a dizer. E com isso, a obra de Deus sofre. E consequentemente se gera cristãos fracos, doentes espirituais, que não tiveram o alimento necessário para crescerem fortes e saudáveis. Em Oséias 4:6 lemos, "O meu povo foi destruído porque lhe faltou o conhecimento".

Aqui nos Estados Unidos e Canadá existem parques de diversões com jardins chamados *Busch Gardens*. Esses lindos jardins são maravilhosos. Quem os visita pode ver a beleza deles, que enche os olhos. Mas, isso só acontece porque há pessoas cuidando, limpando, arrancando as ervas daninhas, colocando adubos adequados pra sua sobrevivência, regando com água limpa e aparando os arbustos. Há um mutirão de pessoas trabalhando para que esses jardins continuem limpos e belos.

Na vida espiritual somos como um jardim que necessita de cuidados. Se não vigiarmos, o inimigo vem e semeia ervas daninhas em nosso caminho sem que percebamos. E em pouco tempo estamos fracos, sem vontade de ler a Bíblia, orar. Participar dos trabalhos na igreja se torna enfadonho, tudo parece nos sufocar. O inimigo é como o bicho preguiça. Ele vai tirando a força do crente pouco a pouco, e você não percebe.

Vai aqui um alerta! Se você começar a ter mais prazer nas coisas do mundo do que nas coisas de Deus, cuidado! Comece logo a botar seu joelho no chão e pedir ao Senhor livramento, fortaleza e misericórdia. O inimigo está só esperando o momento pra levar você a cair nas artimanhas dele.

Quando completei dezessete anos, minha mãe e eu fomos morar no Rio de Janeiro. Saímos do Nordeste para o Sudeste do Brasil. Alguns parentes já estavam no Rio e fomos nos juntar a eles. Eu era uma moça muito bonita e cobiçada pelos rapazes.

Cheguei a ficar noiva e quase me casei. Passamos um tempo na casa de minha prima, depois alugamos nossa própria casa.

Minha mãe foi trabalhar de doméstica e eu fui ser babá em Copacabana, um bairro nobre do Rio de Janeiro, onde tem uma das praias mais bonitas da zona sul. Foi então que começou meu fundo de poço. Ficava de segunda a sexta no trabalho e passava os finais de semana com a família.

Fiz muitas amizades, e sem a supervisão da família. Estava livre para fazer o que quisesse. Só que essa liberdade me custou muito sofrimento.

Copacabana era uma praia linda e cheia de muitos atrativos para uma jovem sem experiência e quase sem maldade. Enfim, eu era ingênua e confiava nas pessoas. Não tinha ninguém para me orientar sobre o mundo de ilusão que passei a conhecer.

Foi nesse paraíso que conheci o Jefferson. Um jovem muito lindo! Era muito parecido com um ator famoso de Hollywood, chamado Tony Curtis. Ele tinha olhos verdes, cabelos negros, pele morena queimada de sol. Era um deus grego!

Eu me encantei com ele. Só tinha um defeito, ele não era alto, mas pra mim isso não importava, eu também era baixinha. Eu achava que estava vivendo um conto de fadas. A gente só se separava para ir trabalhar. Eu estava muito envolvida com ele.

Só não sabia que aquele príncipe era possessivo, violento e se embriagava. No início do nosso namoro, ele não se revelou, só mais tarde.

E quando me dei conta, já estava grávida. Quase tive um ataque quando descobri. O que diria a minha mãe? Porém, Deus é maravilhoso e cuidou de mim. Quando contei ao Jefferson que estava grávida, me disse: “Vamos alugar um canto pra nós morarmos." Dou graças a Deus pelo Jefferson não ter me abandonado e ter aceito a situação.

Mas, não era isso o que eu queria. Fomos morar juntos sem casar, e eu sempre sonhei em me casar. Estava perdido o meu sonho de um casamento na igreja, toda de branco. Naquela época, pra se casar de branco na igreja, não podia estar grávida ou vivendo com parceiro. Casava-se só no juiz, em uma cerimônia simples.

Ele trabalhava num escritório de contabilidade e eu trabalhava em uma sapataria. Morávamos em Copacabana. Nossa casa era compartilhada com outro rapaz pra ajudar a pagar o aluguel.

A situação era muito difícil porque viver na zona Sul era muito caro. Passávamos muitas privações. Muitas vezes precisávamos dividir uma vitamina de abacate ou uma sopa de feijão no jantar. Mas, eu estava feliz. Achava que tinha encontrado a perfeita felicidade.

Nesse tempo da minha primeira gravidez, o Jefferson me tratava com carinho, me ajudava nas tarefas de casa e não ia pra cama sem mim. Éramos muito ligados um ao outro. Tudo parecia perfeito. Eu não sabia que depois que minha filha nascesse, tudo mudaria.

Nasceu a Celeste. Ela era linda! Parecia criança de capa de revista. Uma vez fui parada na rua e uma mocinha perguntou: "O que sua filha come? Ela é tão bonita!" A mãe dela, que estava ao lado, disse: "Ela não é mãe dela! Você não está vendo que é a babá?"

Eu me dediquei àquela linda criança que chegou sem ser planejada, mas que foi muito amada por nós. Até hoje me pergunto o que aconteceu com aquela união feliz e aparentemente tão perfeita.

Cinco anos depois engravidei da Celina. Uma criança raquítica, com baixo peso e muito chorona. Mas, muito amada também por nós. Quando acabava de mamar, eu a colocava na palma da mão para arrotar. Então ela me dava o mais lindo sorriso que jamais pude ver. Era muito miudinha, uma boneca.

Antes mesmo do nascimento da Celina, já havia começado os desentendimentos, as brigas e as agressões verbais. Só não aconteciam agressões físicas porque eu ficava calada e só chorava.

Ele me maltratava muito, não queria que minha mãe viesse me ver ou ajudar em alguma tarefa da casa. Eu tinha que lavar, passar, cozinhar, cuidar da casa, das duas filhas e de um sobrinho dele que veio da roça pra morar em nossa casa. Ele não ajudava em nada. Muitas vezes o sobrinho dele, vendo a minha luta, colocava Celina para dormir. Quando ela estava com sono, chorava muito até dormir.

Com essa vida difícil e sem saber o que fazer, fiquei doente. Tive síndrome do pânico, depressão e muito medo. Não dormia porque pensava que se dormisse, não ia acordar. Não podia comer porque tudo me fazia mal. Cheguei a pesar 37 quilos. Tinha medo de tomar remédio. Não via televisão porque tinha medo. Não queria que ninguém me visitasse. Minha vida era um verdadeiro inferno.

Muitas vezes tive vontade de me jogar embaixo de um carro, porém eu olhava para minhas filhas e pensava: "elas vão sofrer muito se eu fizer isso." Deus não permitiu que eu me matasse. Eu as amava muito e não queria que elas sofressem com a minha morte. Vejo hoje que era Deus cuidando de mim.

A Palavra do Senhor em Eclesiastes 8:11, diz: "Visto como se não executa logo o juízo sobre a má obra, por isso o coração dos filhos dos homens está inteiramente disposto para praticar o mal."

Eu estava colhendo o resultado do meu pecado—da minha rebeldia. Pecado de ter me afastado dos caminhos do Senhor. De ter ido consultar cartomantes, horóscopos e coisas de ocultismo, feitiçaria. De ter aproveitado o que o mundo oferece. Porque não dei ouvidos à palavra santa e pura do nosso amado Salvador Jesus Cristo, passei por muitas aflições e desespero. Não desejo a ninguém o que eu sofri, o que passei nas mãos do diabo. Amado, não troque Jesus por nada. Não vale a pena. Só Nele há paz, alegria e a perfeita felicidade. Não deixe Jesus fora de sua vida.

6

TENTANDO VOLTAR AO PRIMEIRO AMOR

Depois que eu me desviei, até quis voltar pra Jesus, mas não tinha forças. Eu estava presa pelos ardis do adversário. Passei trinta anos longe da presença de Deus. Com todo o sofrimento que passei, ainda levei um longo tempo pra eu compreender que precisava voltar para Jesus.

Deus é maravilhoso, longânimo e compassivo. E as Suas misericórdias são a causa de não sermos consumidos. Ele sempre está pronto a nos dar a oportunidade de reconhecermos nossos erros, nos arrependermos e voltarmos para Sua presença. Ele sempre dá uma segunda chance.

Meu retorno para a presença de Deus foi muito doloroso, porque satanás não queria me perder e fez de tudo para me oprimir com medos, doenças e problemas.

Glórias a Deus porque quando escolhe alguém, ninguém pode tirar das mãos Dele. Em Isaías 43:13 lemos, "Ainda antes que houvesse dia, Eu Sou; e ninguém há que possa fazer escapar das minhas mãos: operando Eu, quem impedirá?" Foi o que aconteceu comigo quando me decidi por Jesus de fato e de verdade. Foi conversão verdadeira. Porém, eu voltei pela dor.

Se você que está lendo este livro está afastado do Senhor, não espere voltar pela dor. Venha por amor! É muito melhor.

Quando me decidi por Jesus eu ainda estava muito debilitada e o Senhor foi me curando gradativamente. Curou-me de uma terrível enxaqueca. Comecei a comer melhor e a dormir melhor. Mas, ainda levou cinco anos para eu me restabelecer completamente

Foram tempos de muita entrega e muita batalha dentro de casa. O Jefferson não aceitava minha nova fé e às vezes chegava bêbado e quebrava as coisas dentro de casa. Certa vez me ameaçou com um revólver e tive que me trancar no banheiro. As crianças ficaram na janela pedindo socorro. Graças a Deus que me deu livramento da fúria daquele homem. Eu vivia com muito medo de acontecer algum mal comigo ou com minhas filhas.

Um domingo estava saindo para a igreja, e ia dar aula na escola dominical, então ele veio me jogou no chão e saiu me arrastando para dentro de casa. Depois fechou a porta e não me deixou sair. A vizinha veio pedir para ele deixar as crianças saírem e tomar um calmante, mas ele não deixou. Ficamos as três sentadas no sofá. Então tive uma ideia.

Comecei a orar baixinho. Ele sentou no outro sofá e quando olhei estava dormindo. Ao acordar, estava calmo e muito envergonhado pelo que havia feito. Depois descobri que ele tinha uma amante e passava as noites fora de casa. Ele não se decidia ficar em casa e deixar a amante ou então ir embora de vez.

E com isso, eu vivia como uma empregada. Pensei em tomar uma posição e tive uma grande ideia. Como ele bebia, resolvi simular que eu estava bêbada, esvaziando a garrafa de cachaça na pia e segurando um copo d'água na mão, quando ele chegou. Ele ficou muito assustado. E falou assim, "Você está maluca? Você não pode beber! Você é crente e vai passar mal." Mas eu estava decidida a dar um susto nele. Além do copo com água e a garrafa, estava com uma faca na mão. Ele tentou tirar a faca de mim, mas eu falei, "Não chegue perto de mim, pois não estou boa da cabeça!" E ele ficou estatelado no sofá e não foi dormir no quarto nesta noite. Quando acordei, ele estava na sala. Depois do susto, ele ficou uma semana com diarréia e resolveu ir embora. E eu depois pedi perdão a Deus por essa atitude tão drástica.

7

ENCONTRANDO O DEUS QUE TUDO PODE

Mesmo enfraquecida por causa dos maus tratos, me matriculei em um curso noturno pra fazer o antigo primeiro grau. Eu tinha estudado apenas até a quarta série do primeiro grau. Felizmente, consegui concluir. Mas, por causa da minha saúde frágil parei o curso várias vezes.

Certa noite, me deitei e quando acordei pela manhã e tentei sentar na cama não consegui, cai para o lado. Era como se meu corpo perdesse o equilíbrio. Não sentava, não levantava e não andava. Busquei todos os especialistas que pude, mas ninguém conseguiu descobrir o que eu tinha. Porém, Jesus já tinha preparado a cura para mim. Glórias a Deus por isso! Ele estava só esperando eu voltar para Ele sem reservas. Porque eu disse: "Ou pra morrer ou pra viver, quero ficar com Jesus."

Por não poder cuidar dos afazeres da casa, eu andava triste. Com duas filhas pequenas pra cuidar, quem iria me ajudar? Não podia pagar uma empregada e o Jefferson dizia que eu não tinha nada, que estava fingindo doença.

Nessa época eu tive um sonho. Sonhei que atendia o telefone e do outro lado alguém dizia: "Eu vim te trazer boas novas." Eu não sabia que a palavra evangelho significa boas novas. Fiquei preocupada e pensei: "Será que vou morrer? Esse telefonema será um aviso do outro mundo pra mim?" Isso eu pensei na minha ignorância espiritual. Quem está no outro mundo não se comunica conosco.

Graças a Deus não morri, mas Deus me deu a segunda chance de conhecê-lo melhor, ter experiências maravilhosas com Ele e ver quão grande Ele é.

No curso que estava fazendo, conheci Marilene e logo ficamos amigas. Essa amiga foi como um anjo enviado por Deus pra minha vida.

Marilene era crente e frequentava um culto de libertação próximo a casa dela. Vindo me visitar me perguntou se eu queria ir a uma reunião de oração perto da minha casa. Eu disse que sim, mas eu não conseguia andar. A irmã dirigente disse pra Marilene que Deus queria que eu fosse lá. Eu falei com Marilene: "Como vou até lá se não estou conseguindo andar?" As irmãs ficaram orando por mim, pra que eu conseguisse ir até lá.

Depois de um mês que Marilene me convidou para o culto de libertação (as irmãs ficaram orando por mim durante todo esse mês), então eu finalmente pude ir ao culto e lá tive um encontro real com Deus, depois da oração.

Eu fui melhorando aos poucos, como disse. Uns cinco anos depois fiquei recuperada. Jesus me salvou, me curou, restaurou minha autoestima e me deu experiências com Ele. Louvado seja o Senhor pela Sua bondade!

Esse era um culto de libertação frequentado por batistas renovados e pentecostais. Terminando o culto, a irmã dirigente fez o apelo, pra quem quisesse aceitar a Jesus como seu Salvador. Eu fiquei quieta no meu canto; só a ouvia dizer: "Aceita Jesus!" Ela continuava falando, "Aceita Jesus!" Aquela insistência foi me irritando. Eu pensei: "Eu vou levantar a mão pra essa mulher calar essa boca!" Ainda ali, eu estava resistindo ao apelo de ir me consertar com Deus. Ele, na sua grande misericórdia, segurou minha mão. Daquele momento em diante, eu estava sob os cuidados do Senhor Jesus Cristo. Aleluia! Levantei minha mão pra Ele. Foi a melhor decisão que eu tomei em toda a minha vida.

8

SAINDO DA ESCURIDÃO

Quando eu tive aquele encontro com Jesus naquele culto, eu ainda estava vivendo com meu companheiro, com quem vivi durante vinte e um anos. Só me firmei com o Senhor dois anos antes do pai das minhas filhas ir embora.

Quando Jefferson descobriu que eu estava indo para a igreja, começou a me perseguir. Então começaram as outras provações. Ele não queria que eu fosse aos cultos. Eu tinha que ir escondida.

Amados, foram muitas as perseguições. Ele dizia que eu ia atrás do pastor. Quando faltava algo em casa e eu falava com ele, e a resposta era: "Vai pedir ao pastor." Mas, eu perseverei em buscar a Deus. Jesus me deu vitória! Aleluia! Eu estava muito apaixonada por Jesus. Aonde ia, levava folhetos e contava o que Ele tinha feito por mim. Como tinha tido misericórdia de mim.

Passei a ser dizimista e ofertante depois de três meses que estava cultuando com as irmãs. A dirigente me chamava para fazer visitas com ela, me dava oportunidade de louvar e até orar. Celina se converteu e me acompanhava nas visitas que fazíamos.

Certa vez, sai para fazer visitas com as irmãs. Quando cheguei ao local combinado, elas já tinham ido embora. Voltei para casa. Quando entrei no corredor do meu prédio algumas crianças vieram correndo gritando por socorro. "Tem uma mulher maluca e a gente está com medo de ir para casa!" Fui ver o que estava acontecendo. Essa senhora tinha sido empregada de uma vizinha do nosso prédio. Eu me aproximei e perguntei: "O que está acontecendo, dona Maria?" E a resposta veio de uma voz estranha: "Eu não sou dona Maria! O que você está fazendo aqui? As trevas não se unem com a luz." Olhei para trás pra ver se havia mais alguém. Não havia mais ninguém além da minha filha Celina.

Compreendi que aquela senhora estava possessa por espíritos malignos. Eu não tinha experiência em expulsar demônios (exorcismo ou libertação). Em minha pouca sabedoria eu ordenei, em nome do Senhor Jesus, que aquela entidade saísse. Aquela senhora caiu no chão e deu muito trabalho para aqueles demônios saírem. Eram muitos.

Chegou um momento que eles disseram, "Vamos levá-la para a rua e jogá-la embaixo do carro." Então eu disse, "Estão amarrados com as mãos para trás."

Ela botou as mãos para trás como se estivesse fisicamente amarrada. Eu estava ficando cansada de tanto mandar aqueles demônios embora e eles voltarem. Ou então, eram muitos. De repente tive uma ideia. Perguntei: "O que vocês estão fazendo ai?" Os espíritos respoderam, "Ela vai à igreja e depois vai à macumba pedir para arranjar marido."

Por causa daquela mistura, ficou oprimida. E trouxe aquela situação pra vida dela. Abrindo porta para o inimigo entrar. Finalmente, as irmãs souberam o que estava acontecendo e vieram me ajudar. Com muita luta, depois de algum tempo, aquela senhora foi liberta. Glórias a Deus por isso!

Amados, tenham muito cuidado se vocês vão procurar ajuda num lugar que não seja na Casa de Deus. Você está se expondo à problemas maiores ainda. Quando precisar, procure ajuda de Deus, com pessoas que realmente estão preparadas para orarem por você.

No Salmo 46:1 diz, "Deus é o nosso refúgio e fortaleza, socorr bem presente na angústia." Só Nele você encontrará o socorro nas suas necessidades.

9

SERVINDO A UM DEUS TREMENDO

Nessa minha trajetória, depois que me firmei nos caminhos do Senhor, tenho sido usada por Jesus no ministério da Palavra. Já tomei conta de uma igreja como pastora, trabalhei como professora, evangelista de crianças (por três anos e meio em minha casa). Fui também presidente das senhoras, diaconisa e também fui consagrada como missionária. Já cantei em coral, inclusive nos Estados Unidos. Cantei num coral em que meu genro era regente. Tenho sido usada pela misericórdia de Deus no ministério de intercessão. Tenho visto Deus operar grandemente na minha vida. Louvado seja Deus!

Deus cuidou de mim quando Jefferson me abandonou depois de 21 anos vivendo juntos. Foram dias muito difíceis de tremenda escassez.

Eu que havia me acostumado a ter a mesa farta, carro do ano e casa na praia, mas agora não tinha praticamente o que comer. Voltei a trabalhar como balconista numa loja de tecidos, mas o salário era muito pouco para nós três. Mal dava para pagar as compras. Ele foi viver com uma moça mais jovem que a filha dele. Estava tão envolvido com ela que acabou esquecendo completamente das filhas e de mim. Só se preocupava em satisfazer aos caprichos daquela mulher. Certa vez ele me disse: "Você não serve para mim. Está muito santa."

Um dia eu estava muito triste porque faltava tudo em casa. Então, veio uma irmã que tinha o dom de profecia para orar por mim. Usada pelo Senhor, ela disse: "Eu sou o teu pastor, nada vai te faltar." Eu fiz como Sara, duvidei. Eu disse: "Nada vai me faltar, é?"

O parceiro que era o provedor da casa foi embora. Não deixou pensão e não queria saber das privações que eu e as crianças estávamos passando. O sofrimento e a tristeza obscureceram a minha visão espiritual. Não conseguia enxergar a grandeza desse Deus maravilhoso e que não há nada impossível para Ele.

Numa noite em que estava cansada, desolada de passar tantas necessidades, fui até a janela e olhei para o céu. Então comecei a conversar com Deus.

Eu tenho esse hábito de conversar com Deus. E a conversa foi assim: "Senhor, eu não aguento mais comer sardinha," era a única coisa que eu conseguia comprar com o que ganhava. "Eu queria comer um bife, mas não tenho dinheiro pra comprar. Quando aquele homem vivia aqui eu comia bife de filé mignon, e agora só como sardinha. Eu vou à feira quando já está na hora de desarmarem as barracas para comprar os restos, porque é mais barato. Não suporto mais isso!"

Quando fiz esse desabafo já eram vinte e três horas e eu fui dormir. Ao acordar no dia seguinte, uma das irmãs do grupo de oração que eu frequentava e gostava muito de mim, me ligou. Ela morava perto da minha casa. "Minha filha, você já comeu?", ela perguntou. "Não," respondi. "Então venha aqui em casa," ela pediu.

Eu fui bem rápido. Ao chegar lá, ela disse para eu estender a minha mão para ela. Ela colocou uma nota em minha mão, e disse, "Tome este dinheiro pra você."

Espantada eu perguntei: "Porque?" E Ela disse, "Foi Jesus que mandou eu lhe dar esse dinheiro pra você comprar um bife pra você comer."

"Quem disse à senhora que eu queria comer bife?", eu perguntei. "Foi Jesus. Ele me disse 'dá esse dinheiro pra minha serva comprar bife para comer'," ela explicou.

Eu fiquei admirada e comovida com o cuidado que o Senhor teve comigo. Desse dia em diante eu tive a certeza que Deus é vivo e real. Ele vê tudo o que acontece conosco e está pronto para atender ao desejo do nosso coração. Eu não falei com ninguém, só com Ele e fui dormir. Fiquei maravilhada com essa experiência tão grandiosa que vivenciei. Sempre que posso, conto esse testemunho para a glória de Deus.

Outra experiência que tive foi: Celeste estudava em uma faculdade, fazia Letras. E sempre que tinha prova precisava pagar. Ela se esqueceu de me avisar. Eu não tinha dinheiro, o pai não tinha deixado. Se ela não pagasse, teria que fazer segunda chamada e o preço seria maior.

Em minha casa dinheiro era sempre motivo de briga, discussões. E eu fazia de tudo para viver em paz. Então pensei: "vou à casa de uma amiga oferecer à venda um arranjo de flores que tenho aqui em casa." Fui, mas não a encontrei. Ofereci a outra senhora que não quis.

Voltei para casa triste e cabisbaixa, pensando: "Meu Deus, vai ter mais briga quando aquele homem chegar em casa, à noite." Vinha olhando para o chão, mas tinha um carro parado do meu lado esquerdo. Como achei que conhecia as pessoas que estavam no carro, me abaixei para cumprimentá-las. Vi que não conhecia ninguém. Mas, mais adiante, ao abaixar pra olhar dentro do carro, vi que na rua havia um bolo de dinheiro amassado. Peguei aquele dinheiro bem rápido, e vim pra casa, gritando. Ao entrar em casa estava agitada e gritando: "Celeste, olha aqui o dinheiro. Achei na rua. Deus é bom!"

Aconteceu que pessoas que me deviam também foram me pagar naquele dia. Celeste teve o dinheiro para pagar a prova e ainda sobrou.

"Lança o teu cuidado sobre o Senhor e Ele te susterá,
nunca permitirá que o justo seja abalado"
(Salmo 55:22).

Em outra época, quando estava nos Estados Unidos trabalhando como baby-sitter de um garoto, tive outra experiência impactante. Eu passava a semana no trabalho e finais de semana ficava com a família. Lembro-me que fui ao supermercado e lá vi uns pêssegos grandes e bonitos. Vale ressaltar que pêssego é minha fruta predileta. Eles estavam de dar água na boca, porém estava com pouco dinheiro naquele dia. Além disso, estava economizando. Só gastava o necessário. Porém, a vontade de comer os pêssegos era grande, mas não comprei.

Chegou sexta-feira e fui para a casa da minha filha. Estávamos conversando na cozinha, e foi quando Celina abriu a geladeira. Tirou de lá um pêssego e veio com ele em minha direção estendendo-o para mim. Eu disse intrigada, "Por que você está me dando esse pêssego?" "Mãe", ela respondeu, "eu ia comer esse pêssego, mas na hora que eu levei à boca, Deus me disse para não comer e guardar para a senhora."

Eu olhei pra ela agradecendo a Deus pela sua bondade. Eu queria comer pêssego, mas como estava caro, não comprei. Deus usou minha filha para me dar o que eu queria comer.

"Deleita-te também no Senhor e ele te concederá o que deseja o teu coração" (Salmo 37:4).

Amados, não resta a menor dúvida, **Deus se preocupa com aqueles que lhe pertencem.**

> Olhai para as aves do céu, que nem semeiam nem segam, nem ajuntam em celeiros; e vosso Pai celestial as alimenta. Não tendes vós muito mais valor do que elas? (Mateus 6:26).

10

LIVRE PARA SERVIR JESUS

Quando Jefferson foi embora, procurei me ocupar mais em aprender sobre Deus. Fiz um curso de pregador leigo. Fiz comunicação visual, mas não assimilei bem porque sou ruim em desenho. Fiz curso de professora evangelista de crianças. Entrei no coral da igreja. Eu queria estar ocupada na obra do Senhor.

Participava dos cultos de libertação com minha filha mais nova, Celina. Celeste se converteu mais tarde. Para a glória de Deus, as duas servem ao Senhor.

Celeste fez o Seminário Teológico Batista do Sul do Brasil no Rio de Janeiro e é professora da Escola Bíblica Dominical. É muito usada no ministério da Palavra. É também formada pela APEC e tem sido muito usada por Deus com os adolescentes. Celina toca violão acústico, canta e também ministra lá em Washington, D.C., onde vive.

Depois que Celina foi viver nos Estados Unidos, Celeste se casou aqui no Brasil com um empresário do ramo de tintas e me deu duas lindas netas. Kate, a mais velha, é morena e mais parece uma modelo. É casada e vive no Texas, EUA. Ela e seu esposo tem uma linda bebê. Quando criança foi capa de revista. Foi mensageira do Rei e liderou o grupo de mocidade quando estava aqui no Brasil. Julice, a mais nova, também é casada com um micro empresário. É uma loirinha muito graciosa e também foi capa de revista. Julice e seu esposo Gilson me presentearam com três lindas bisnetas.

O ano de 1986 foi muito difícil para mim. Celeste havia se casado, meu marido já tinha ido embora de casa e eu estava ficando cada vez mais sozinha. Celina, minha companheira na obra, já estava mocinha. Precisava ter amigos da idade dela. Como ela tocava e cantava, minha casa vivia cheia de jovens. Ela também era muito bonita. Que trabalho me deu por causa dos admiradores!

Nesse ano (1986), vários batistas americanos vieram ao Brasil para evangelizar no Rio de Janeiro. Era uma grande cruzada e nossa igreja recebeu uma delegação vinda da Carolina do Norte. Como faltou intérprete, minha filha Celina trabalhou ajudando na interpretação para o grupo de americanos. O problema era que ela não tinha experiência em traduzir sermões do púlpito, mas graças a Deus saiu-se bem.

Ela fez amizade com um dos integrantes do grupo chamado Paulo. Ele era muito brincalhão e todos gostaram muito dele. Paulo era casado, mas não tinha filhos. Ele admirou tanto o potencial da minha filha que decidiu pagar uma faculdade pra ela na América do Norte.

Quando eu soube que Celina estava querendo ir para Estados Unidos, morar com uma família que eu não conhecia e viver numa terra cuja língua eu não falava, fiquei apavorada. E se minha filha tivesse problemas? Eu não teria como socorrê- la. Eu não tinha dinheiro para ir buscá-la, não falava a língua. Posso dizer que entrei em grande desespero.

Falei com o pai dela pedindo que ele a impedisse de viajar. Ele me respondeu: "Você está doida? Eu não vou impedir o futuro da menina."

Então fui pedir ao pastor dela que era advogado. Ele me disse: "Se a senhora não permitir, eu assino a permissão para a menina viajar." Todos achavam que ela devia ir. Eu não queria de jeito nenhum, mas essa viagem estava determinada por Deus.

Depois de uns quatro meses que o Paulo esteve aqui em minha casa, voltou com sua esposa. Eles se hospedaram conosco por quinze dias para me conhecer, conhecer a Celina, nossos hábitos e ver como era o comportamento da minha filha. Voltaram com a promessa de pagar os estudos, cuidar dela dando casa e comida.

E eles cumpriram a promessa. Cuidaram dela como se fosse filha e ela só saiu da casa deles casada com um americano que conheceu na faculdade. Eles pagaram tudo até os telefonemas que ela dava pra mim.

Minha filha formou-se Mestre em Comércio Exterior, e também é licensiada como Despachante alfandegária. Hoje é cidadã americana, e vive há vinte e nove anos em Washington, D.C. com o esposo e os dois filhos, Jonathan e Kevin.

Eu não sabia que Deus estava preparando a minha ida também para os Estados Unidos. Quando estava faltando quinze dias para Celina viajar, Deus falou com uma irmã profetisa para vir à minha casa conversar comigo sobre a viagem da minha filha. Essa profetisa era de uma Assembleia de Deus perto da minha casa. Só que ela não sabia meu nome, nem onde eu morava. Ela veio pela rua perguntando onde morava uma senhora cuja filha ia para os Estados Unidos e que estava muito aflita. Perguntou aqui e ali até que alguém indicou minha casa pra ela.

Chegando aqui, ela falou: "Deus me mandou aqui para te dar um recado. Ele manda te dizer pra você não se preocupar com a viagem de sua filha. É Ele quem está levando sua filha para aquele país. Ela vai como um vaso de honra para uma obra e depois você também vai pra lá."

Depois de alguns anos, quando meu primeiro neto Kevin estava para nascer, eu fui pra lá. Cumpriu-se o recado que o Senhor tinha mandado pra mim. Desde então, tenho vivido no Brasil e nos Estados Unidos.

Deus tem cuidado de mim de uma maneira toda especial. Eu glorifico a Ele por tudo o que Ele fez e ainda faz por mim.

11

BABYSITTER NA TERRA DO TIO SAM

Minha experiência em cuidar de crianças vem desde o tempo em que eu era muito jovem. Meu primeiro emprego foi como babá no Rio de Janeiro. Tenho muita prática em cuidar de crianças. Eu me senti privilegiada de conseguir um trabalho fazendo o que eu gostava de fazer. Pra ser babá nos EUA tem que ser recomendada. É muita responsabilidade. Tem criança que você não pode dizer "não" pra ela. Tem que tomar muito cuidado pra criança não se machucar ou reclamar de você.

Em Washington, D.C., tomei conta dos meus netos e também de muitas outras crianças. Filhos de brasileiros e de americanos. Cuidei de uma garota filha de um militar de alto escalão do Pentágono.

Foi o trabalho mais difícil que encontrei porque nem ele nem a esposa falavam português, minha língua nativa. Porém Jesus me deu graça e eu fiquei lá mais de um ano. Quando eu precisava me comunicar usava o dicionário ou pedia para Celina ser minha intérprete.

As mães viviam me telefonando querendo contratar meus serviços porque eu sabia entreter as crianças, por ser evangélica e porque é chique ter uma babá estrangeira. Eu ensinava musiquinhas de Jesus para elas.

Nesse emprego, Deus me deu uma experiência tremenda com Ele. Era verão, época de tornados. Eu estava brincando com a menina quando de repente apareceu a mãe na sala. Ela era branquinha, mas estava mais branca do que era e eu perguntei em inglês o que estava acontecendo. Ela respondeu em inglês: "tornado!" Ela comentou que o tornado estaria passando em quinze minutos sobre nossa casa. Aqui nos Estados Unidos, os tornados destroem tudo por onde passam.

Arrancam árvores, derrubam casas, enfim causam grande estrago. Eu disse a ela para segurar minha mão e orarmos. Ela entendeu o que eu queria dizer. Orei mais ou menos assim (não lembro exatamente porque faz muito tempo que aconteceu): "Repreendo esse tornado! Não vai causar nenhum mal em nome de Jesus!"

Aguardamos porque quando o tornado passa faz um barulho ensurdecedor. Tinhamos que procurar abrigo. No entanto, estava tudo calmo, e então perguntei: "Cadê o tornado?" Ao que ela respondeu: "Não sei. Parece que passou longe daqui." Glórias a Deus pelo grande livramento que nos deu naquela tarde de verão!

Lembro-me também quando Celina estava grávida do Kevin. Estava no oitavo mês de gravidez. Eu estava lá para ajudar quando o neném chegasse. Estávamos conversando e de repente ficou tudo escuro. Era sinal de uma grande tempestade. Meu genro estava vendo televisão e disse: "Vamos para o porão!" Perguntei por quê. Ele disse: "Está vindo um tornado e vai passar por aqui." Comecei a ficar com medo. Peguei meus documentos, uns cobertores e fomos lá pra baixo, onde era o lugar mais seguro da casa.

Eu só pensava que Celina poderia ficar muito nervosa e meu neto nascer antes do tempo. No entanto, sabia que existe um Deus que tem o controle do universo na palma de suas mãos. E que tem poder para acalmar qualquer tempestade.

Procurei um lugar onde podia avistar o céu e clamei: "Senhor, desvia esse tornado para bem longe daqui. Para que não venha causar nenhum mal a nós." Terminando de orar, voltei ao lugar onde estava antes e fiquei aguardando. Um pouco depois meu genro gritou lá de cima: "Já podem subir! O tornado passou há uma hora e meia daqui. E lá onde passou causou um grande estrago."

Enquanto estava lá ouvi uma história de um tornado muito forte. A força dele era tanta que chegou a arrancar um bebezinho dos braços da mãe. Depois esse bebê foi encontrado com vida enganchado numa árvore. Soubemos que os pais da criança eram crentes. O inimigo muitas vezes tenta arrancar o que nos pertence, o que é nosso. Mas Deus cuida e nos devolve. Louvado seja Deus! Lembra-se de Jó? Ele perdeu os dez filhos, tudo o que tinha. Depois, Deus devolveu tudo a ele em dobro.

"E abençoou o Senhor o último estado de Jó mais do que o primeiro." (Jó 42:12)

12

EXPERIÊNCIA COM A NEVE

Eu estava em outro estado tomando conta de uma linda menina loira filha de mãe brasileira e pai americano. Vinha pra casa na sexta-feira à noite e na segunda-feira de manhã voltava para o trabalho. Tinha que pegar o metrô e atravessar várias estações fazendo conexões de uma linha para outra.

Era domingo à tarde quando a dona da casa me ligou dizendo: "Venha hoje porque eu vou precisar da senhora amanhã bem cedo." Eu fiquei preocupada porque a televisão e o rádio estavam anunciando muita neve para aquela noite. Eu disse a ela: "Não posso. Vai cair muita neve hoje. É possível que pare o metrô e fique perigoso para eu chegar ai." Ela respondeu: "Venha de qualquer jeito. Eu preciso da senhora aqui!"

Então orei ao Senhor e pedi que durante o tempo que eu levasse para chegar a casa dela não caísse nenhum floco de neve. Fui orando.

Ao chegar à última estação do metrô o carro já estava me esperando. Fomos rápido para casa. Chegando lá, subi para o quarto e troquei de roupa. Ao olhar pela janela o chão já estava branquinho de neve. "Uau!", exclamei. Enquanto eu estava a caminho da casa não caiu nem um floquinho de neve. Às vezes nossa fé é fraca e não cremos na oração que fazemos. Jesus "segurou" aquela neve e me protegeu até que eu chegasse, em segurança. Louvado seja Deus por Sua proteção!

Tive outras experiências com Deus. Eu estava cuidando de dois meninos. O mais velho estava na escola e eu tinha que buscá-lo no ponto do ônibus escolar, à tarde. Naquele dia estava desabando uma grande tempestade. Choveu o dia todo. Uma chuva pesada. E eu tinha que levar no colo o menino pequeno. A mãe me ligou preocupada. Não podia deixar o pequeno sozinho em casa. Então orei ao Senhor. Pedi que aquela tempestade parasse e eu pudesse pegar a criança sem problema. Trinta minutos antes de o garoto ser deixado no ponto de ônibus escolar, a tempestade cessou e até apareceu o sol. Quando eu contei pra mãe o que havia acontecido, ela ficou espantada. Como poderia aquela tempestade parar exatamente na hora da criança voltar? Foi a graça de Deus para comigo.

> Mas na verdade Deus me ouviu; atendeu a voz da minha oração. Bendito seja Deus que não rejeitou a minha oração, nem desviou de mim a sua misericórdia (Salmo 66:19-20).

Lembro-me do profeta Elias que era um homem sujeito às mesmas paixões que nós. Ele estava aborrecido pelo que o rei Acabe andava fazendo. Ele disse: "Vive o Senhor, Deus de Israel, perante cuja face estou, que nestes anos nem orvalho nem chuva haverá senão segundo a minha palavra." (1 Reis 17:13) E Deus ouviu a palavra de Elias. Israel sofreu uma grande seca. A palavra da pessoa que teme a Deus tem poder.

Você deve estar se perguntando por que eu mudava tanto de trabalho. Como eu não falava inglês fluente ficava com crianças que ainda eram pequenas. Quando elas iam crescendo os pais preferiam colocá-las no pre-escolar. Uma espécie de Jardim de Infância com muitas atividades para crianças pequenas. Elas estavam aprendendo a falar, precisavam aprender a língua delas.

Eu estava em outra casa perto da casa da minha filha Celina. Nesse trabalho eu só cuidava de um lindo garotinho. Ele era muito bonzinho. Eu amei muito todas as crianças que Deus colocou no meu caminho para cuidar. Quando tinha que ir, saía chorando. Tenho fotos de quase todos eles.

Eu e Celina tínhamos o hábito de orar pelo telefone. Eu estava no meu celular orando com ela quando de repente apagou. Pensei que precisasse carregar a bateria, mas não era isso. Então declarei que não ia gastar dinheiro consertando aquele celular. Mais tarde voltei a checar e ele continuava apagado. De madrugada orei pelo celular e no dia seguinte à tarde ele voltou a funcionar normalmente. Para honra e glória do Senhor.

Eu sempre vinha nos finais de semana ficar com minha família. Meu neto Kevin pedia pra dormir perto de mim e claro que eu permitia. Uma noite, todos já dormiam, devia ser uma hora da madrugada, quando Kevin começou com uma tosse. Não havia nada que parasse aquela tosse. Ele é branquinho, mas teve uma hora que ele olhou pra mim todo vermelho e suado. Pensei: "Senhor, o que posso fazer?" Então clamei ao Deus do céu, repreendi aquela tosse e imediatamente a tosse foi embora.

Deus curou o meu genro, esposo de Celina, de uma alergia a uma erva daninha que deixou seus braços e barriga em carne viva. Ele nem conseguia colocar a roupa. Nessa experiência Celina orou comigo.

Em outra ocasião, nossa família veio ao Brasil passar férias. Alugamos uma casa porque era bastante gente. Estávamos nos preparando para fazermos uma visita. Minha filha foi dar banho no Jonathan. De repente ouvi gritos. Encontrei minha filha parada, meu genro branco, sem fala. Meu neto tinha caído e estava com um corte profundo acima da nuca. Quando vi aquela cena corri e coloquei minha mão em cima do corte. Orei, o sangramento parou e em pouco tempo o menino estava bem, correndo e fazendo arte. Não precisou ir ao pronto socorro. De fato, como era um lugar remoto, não havia como socorrê-lo rapidamente. Jesus o curou. Aleluia! Glórias a Deus pela sua bondade!

Jesus tem sido fiel na minha vida e quando olho para trás vejo de onde Jesus me tirou. Só tenho que glorificá-lo por tudo o que Ele fez por mim. Tenho viajado sozinha para os Estados Unidos e para o Brasil dentro de um avião. Isso realmente é um milagre, considerando que já sofri com a Síndrome do Pânico.

13

MEU PRIMEIRO EMPREGO EM D.C.

Eu estava procurando trabalho. Meu neto não estava precisando mais dos meus cuidados. Resolvi trabalhar. Nos Estados Unidos, especialmente em Washington, a vida é muito cara e eu não queria depender financeiramente da minha filha.

Conversando com ela, decidimos colocar um anúncio na igreja oferecendo meus serviços de babá, porque era o que eu sabia fazer muito bem, tomar conta de crianças. Lá se costuma fazer isso. Coloca-se anúncio nas igrejas evangélicas oferecendo ou buscando trabalho.

Um casal de pastores de uma grande igreja viu meu anúncio e me convidaram pra entrevista. Esse casal era de classe média alta. Moravam num bairro nobre da cidade. Eles tinham morado um tempo no Brasil e adotaram duas crianças brasileiras. Uma menina e um menino que já estavam grandes. A família queria uma pessoa que falasse português com eles. Era um tipo de educadora, pra eles não perderem seu contato com a língua. Eles amavam o Brasil e os brasileiros também.

Eu fiquei preocupada em assumir uma posição de educadora. Porém, o meu curso da APEC me ajudou bastante. Enfim, eles gostaram de mim e eu gostei deles. Então fui contratada. O meu trabalho na casa era mais pra falar português, organizar o cardápio e ver o que estava precisando arrumar. A casa tinha três andares e com a bagunça que os meninos faziam, tinha muito o que organizar.

Eles tinham quatro filhos, dois adotivos e dois biológicos. Os dois biológicos eram grandes, estavam na Faculdade morando fora. Só vinham pra casa nas festas, dia de Ação de Graças ou Natal. A dona da casa, a Sara, se tornou minha amiga.

E muitas vezes eu sentava na beirada da cama dela pra ouvir seus desabafos e confortá-la. Felizmente, ela falava e entendia o meu português.

Sara era uma mulher de muita classe. Só vivia fazendo eventos pra arrecadar fundos pra obras da igreja. E nesses eventos ela convidava a alta sociedade americana, oferecendo jantares elegantes. Imagine quem ela convidava pra sentar à mesa da presidente: eu.

Ela fazia questão que eu sentasse com eles ou ao lado do irmão dela, que era divorciado. Luís era muito simpático comigo. E de vez em quando aparecia lá em casa com a desculpa de tomar um café ou para aprender alguma palavra em português.

Lembro-me de uma vez que Sara contratou um cozinheiro pra fazer comida francesa. Ela me disse: "A senhora vai à recepção." Deixei-a ir à frente e me tranquei em meu quarto. Ela me procurou lá, não me viu, então veio em casa me buscar.

Chegando lá, me apresentou para as pessoas. Eu só dizia: "Nice to meet you." Que quer dizer em inglês, "muito prazer." Era assim mesmo que eu falava. Eu me sentia um peixe fora d'água no meio daquele povo chique. Posso dizer que não comi nada naquele jantar. Passei tudo para o Luís, que estava gostando que me servissem, depois dava pra ele. Só comi pão francês e salada naquele dia. Quando cheguei em casa eu fui fazer um lanchinho, pois estava com fome.

Sara gostava muito de mim e eu dela também. Sara era muito especial pra mim. Quando eu caí da escada, porque escorreguei, quebrando a costela (só vim descobrir que tinha quebrado a costela um mês depois quando fui ao médico), ela contratou uma empregada pra fazer o trabalho, não queria que eu fizesse nada. Graças a Deus, Jesus me curou dessa costela quebrada.

Enquanto minha mãe estava viva, eu não quis ser residente nesse país, assim eu passava seis meses nos EUA e um ano no Brasil. Depois que Deus a chamou, então resolvi aceitar ser residente dos EUA. Atualmente estou vivendo no Texas, na cidade de San Antonio e congrego numa igreja Batista de língua hispana. Sempre que posso vou a Washington rever os amigos que tenho por lá.

Amados, eu contei aqui que frequentei lugares da mais alta classe, porém isso pra mim não mudou a minha maneira de ser simples. E quero continuar sendo simples, não ambicionando coisas grandes. Muitas vezes, elas vêm as minhas mãos sem que eu as procure. Gosto desse versículo que diz em Deuteronômio 28:2, "E todas as bençãos virão sobre ti e te alcançarão, quando ouvires a voz do Senhor teu Deus." A recompensa de Deus é o nosso maior tesouro.

Obrigada, Senhor por tudo que tens feito por mim!

14

DIZIMISTA E OFERTANTE

Sou grata a Deus pelos milagres que ele tem operado em minha vida. Sou grata pela Sua provisão porque tem me sustentado em todas as minhas necessidades. Ele tem dado mais do que eu tenho pedido ou pensado.

Hoje, graças a Jesus, tenho roupas e sapatos para dar até aos que precisam. Sempre faço doações porque às vezes preciso de espaço e também ganho muitas coisas. O tempo em que não tinha roupas para vestir, ficou para trás. Louvado seja Deus!

Desde que me firmei no Senhor, Jesus converteu meu coração para ser dizimista fiel e ofertante na obra Dele. Sempre que posso, socorro os irmãos que estão mais necessitados. Em minha vida se cumpre a palavra "é dando que se recebe." Não que eu faça isso na intenção de receber algo em troca. A benção de repartir é que está inserida em mim; deve ser pelo fato de ter passado tantas necessidades tempos atrás e agora eu tenho com fartura. E vejo tanta gente necessitada... Isso me comove.

Mais bem-aventurada coisa é dar do que receber (Atos 20:35b). Por isso, sempre que você puder, doe alguma coisa. Seja generoso. Doe uma palavra de ânimo àquele que está desanimado. Doe um sorriso. Doe um abraço sincero. Leve esperança ao que está aflito. Diga que Jesus o ama. Doe perdão. Você verá como vai se sentir leve.

Gostaria de contar a minha experiência com o perdão. Aconteceu com a amante do meu marido. Eu soube por ele que ela tinha muita raiva de mim. Eu não tinha feito nada para ela, mas ela me odiava. Essa pessoa me causou um grande mal, destruindo minha família. Porém, Jesus me mandou ir até ela e pedir perdão. Eu disse, "Jesus, eu não vou! Ela é quem tem que pedir perdão a mim." Porém, o Senhor Jesus me ordenou, "Vai e peça perdão à ela!" E eu fui, e perguntei se ela tinha algo contra mim, e ela disse que sim, por causa de uma palavra que eu havia dito. Então, eu pedi que ela me perdoasse, e que não era a minha intenção de ofendê-la.

Em seguida, dei-lhe um grande abraço. O rosto dela se irradiou e eu saí dali muito leve, me sentindo livre.

EPÍLOGO

Ao terminar essa história, gostaria de compartilhar com vocês mais um pouquinho da minha trajetória. Estava em San Antonio, ao atender o telefone era o Jefferson. Ele me disse: "Quando você vem ao Brasil?" Eu respondi: "Em breve. Por quê?"

"Preciso conversar sobre nós," ele respondeu. Isso depois de trinta anos separados. Ele queria falar sobre nós?! Fiquei pensando: "O que esse homem está querendo, meu Deus?" Já fazia mais de dez anos que ele estava sozinho. Com sozinho, quero dizer, não tinha pessoas vivendo com ele. Então me disse: "Vamos fazer uma união estável pra você ter direito aos meus bens. Porque você é a única pessoa que merece compartilhar da minha herança." Eu disse a ele: "eu não sei o que é isso, porém vou orar." Despedi-me dele e fui orar e procurar saber o que era aquilo que ele estava me propondo.

Vim ao Brasil e soube que união estável é para pessoas que vivem juntas, não casaram, mas assinam um documento provando que estão juntos. Caso um dos cônjuges venha a falecer, o que ficar tem os mesmos direitos de quem é legalmente casado.

Incrivelmente, começaram a mandar minhas contas pra casa dele. Eu estava no Brasil e ele ligou dizendo: "Vou passar ai pra levar a conta do telefone que mandaram aqui pra casa. Não sei por que mandaram sua conta de telefone pra cá!"

Quando ele chegou aqui, disse pra ele: "Não posso fazer isso. Essa união estável não é correta pra mim. Eu não vivo com você há mais de trinta anos." Então ele falou: "Mas já vivemos, temos duas filhas."

"Mas, no momento não vivemos mais. Se eu fizer isso, estarei mentindo. Eu sou serva de Deus, não vou mentir." E continuei orando.

Todos diziam que a união estável era correta, porém eu não me sentia em paz. Eu havia conversado com uma advogada amiga minha. Ela falou assim: "Se ele quer fazer isso, porque vocês não casam?"

Voltei a orar agora dizendo: "Senhor Deus, se queres isso, eu vou falar com ele pra gente se casar. E se ele aceitar, é porque queres."

Novamente uma das contas foi pra casa dele pela segunda vez. Quando ele veio trazendo a conta, então disse a ele: "Por que então a gente não casa?" Ele ficou calado, deu um sorriso maroto, e foi embora. Celeste falou assim: "Ele nunca vai aceitar se casar!"

Depois de quinze dias que lancei a proposta, ele concordou em casar.

O inimigo lutou até o fim para impedir o nosso casamento. Fomos dar entrada nos papéis e precisávamos de duas testemunhas. Chegamos em frente à escrivã, que é a pessoa que processa os documentos. Tudo correu bem comigo. Quando chegou a vez do Jefferson, a moça disse, "Esse documento aqui não é o seu, é de outra pessoa." Ele havia levado a certidão do filho dele. Então ele voltou em casa para buscar o documento correto. Eu fui em casa para esperar por ele e irmos juntos ao cartório. Foi aí que uma das testemunhas me ligou avisando que ia trabalhar e não poderia esperar a volta do Jefferson na parte da tarde.

Eu literalmente só faltei arrancar os cabelos! Onde eu iria encontrar outra pessoa pra ser minha testemunha de casamento em 30 minutos, antes do cartório fechar, e que tivesse com todos os documentos corretos?

Comecei a ligar pra várias pessoas, e diziam: "O quê? Quem vai casar?" E eu respondia, "Depois eu explico. Não há tempo para explicar agora." Enfim, consegui a testemunha que precisava e marcamos a data da cerimônia. Eu cheguei primeiro e depois uma das testemunhas teve que sair para fazer uma entrevista de trabalho, e não pode comparecer.

Novamente eu estava buscando alguém em cima da hora pra ser minha testemunha do casamento. Não achando ninguém disponível, minha filha Celeste se ofereceu e assim fomos para o cartório celebrar a tão sonhada bodas do Mister Jefferson e Miss Mira. Chegamos lá e quando íamos à presença da juíza, a mestre de cerimônia disse: "O Sr. não pode casar assim; está de bermuda." Então, eu fiquei lá com os convidados e Celeste saiu com ele para comprar umas calças para ele poder se casar. Parece engraçado, mas foi bem difícil pra mim, depois de tudo o que passei, e ainda ter que aguentar isso lá no cartório. Disseram que alguém deveria ir com ele porque de repente, ele poderia deixar a noiva esperando. Enfim, ele conseguiu encontrar a calça e agora não tinha mais desculpas. Graças a Deus, deu tudo certo e mais uma vez, Deus me deu a vitória!

Agora entendo porque Deus não permitiu que ninguém, ninguém gostasse de mim. Porque Ele queria que consertássemos uma situação que ficou pendente em nosso passado.

É por isso que eu amo esse Deus. Ele é fiel, guarda o seu povo. Quando Ele determina uma bênção, ninguém pode impedir. Ele não faz nada pela metade e sempre completa a obra que começou.

Em todos os sentidos, Jesus me deu uma segunda chance. E Ele quer fazer o mesmo por você.

APRESENTAÇÃO DA AUTORA

A missionária Mira Sousa atualmente vive no Rio de Janeiro - Brasil. Vem aos EUA com frequência. É membro da Igreja Batista e faz um trabalho social com a comunidade, no ministério de roupas.

No Brasil, é membro da Igreja Jesus Cristo é a Vida. Trabalhou na Escola Bíblica Dominical e atuou no ministério da Palavra. É formada pela APEC—Aliança Pró Evangelização das Crianças. Teve em sua casa uma classe de evangelismo de crianças por mais de três anos. Foi também pastora da Igreja Cristã da Misericórida por três anos e meio. É casada, tem duas filhas, duas netas e dois netos e quatro bisnetas.

Escreveu este livro para honrar e glorificar ao seu Deus. Mas, também para dar seu testemunho e edificar vidas. Para mostrar a você, leitor, o efeito que a oração pode produzir em sua vida também.

Leia Josué 10:12-14.

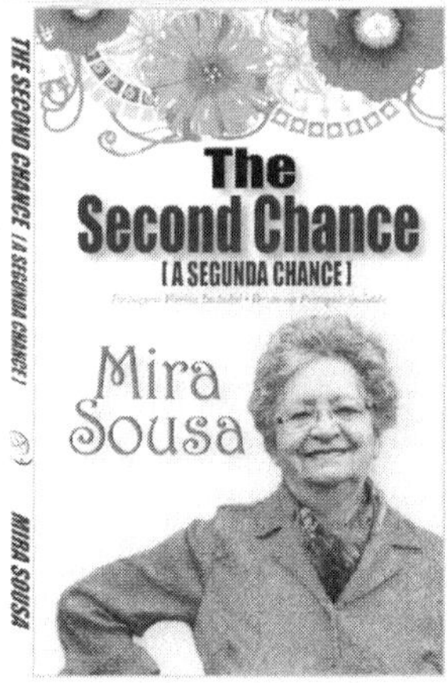

ISBN: 978-1-60273-092-2
Bilingual edition: English & Portuguese

A Segunda Chance
de Missionária Mira Sousa

In ***THE SECOND CHANCE,*** Missionary Mira Sousa shares her life journey which begins as a poor young girl in Brazil. Her life was full of poverty and heartaches where she felt no one in the world cared about her until she came to a saving grace in the Lord Jesus Christ. Mira found out she was not alone and through her faith in God, she would overcome in this life. Prayer—her connection with God—has been her mainstay. Learn about the love of God and the power of prayer through this inspirational story.

ISBN: 978-1-60273-014-4
Edition: Portuguese

A PRIORIDADE DO LOUVOR E ADORAÇÃO
de Dr. Ron Kenoly

Ron Kenoly entrou numa nova temporada em seu ministério onde o seu coração e a sua visão são mentorar líderes de louvor, pastores e adoradores. Através deste livro, você receberá respostas comprovadas às questões comuns e incomuns de um dos líderes e autoridade de louvor mais ungidos e experientes desta nação. Cada capítulo é destinado a levá-lo a um nível mais elevado de excelência e eficácia na sua experiência de adoração.